iPhone 15 Pro

User Guide

Comprehensive Missing User Manual on How to Master the
Device including New iOS Tips and Tricks

Max G. Wilkins

iPhone 15 Pro Phone Guide

All rights reserved. No part of this publication may be reproduced, distributed, or transmitted in any form or by any means, including photocopying, recording, or other electronic or mechanical methods, without the prior written permission of the publisher, except in the case of brief quotations embodied in critical reviews and certain other noncommercial uses permitted by copyright law.

Copyright © 2023.

Table of Contents

Introduction

Welcome to the iPhone 15 Pro User Guide! This thorough guide is meant to help you get the most out of your iPhone 15 Pro by providing you with crucial information, tips, and techniques to improve your smartphone experience.

In this tutorial, we will lead you through the core features and operations of the iPhone 15 Pro, ensuring that you can confidently traverse its possibilities. Whether you're a new iPhone user or upgrading from a prior model, you'll discover helpful insights here.

Before going into the specifications, let's begin with an overview of what makes the iPhone 15 Pro stand out. From its cutting-edge camera system to its strong performance, we'll highlight the major characteristics that make this gadget unique.

Get ready to discover the world of the iPhone 15 Pro and unleash its full potential. Whether you want to shoot great images, keep connected with loved ones, or boost productivity, this guide has you covered. Let's go on this trip together and discover all your iPhone 15 Pro has to offer.

About This Guide

This guide is your go-to reference for understanding and exploiting the iPhone 15 Pro to its best potential. Here's what you can anticipate from this guide:

Comprehensive Coverage: We've arranged this guide to cover all the main parts of your iPhone 15 Pro, from basic setup to advanced functions, ensuring that you have a well-rounded grasp of your device.

User-Friendly Format: We've arranged this tutorial in a user-friendly and easy-to-follow way, with step-by-step directions, screenshots, and suggestions to make your learning experience smooth and pleasurable.

Up-to-date Information: While this guide was developed using the latest available information as of my knowledge cutoff date in September 2021, we suggest checking for any new software upgrades or changes to settings that may have happened after that date.

Troubleshooting Help: We've included a troubleshooting section to aid you in resolving typical difficulties that may develop when using your iPhone 15 Pro, along with practical solutions.

Other Resources: At the conclusion of this tutorial, you'll find a list of other resources, including websites, forums, and Apple's official support channels, where you may seek more help and keep informed on the newest developments.

Whether you're new to the iPhone ecosystem or want to leverage the potential of your iPhone 15 Pro, this guide is here to equip you with the information you need. Let's dig in and make your iPhone 15 Pro experience both pleasurable and productive.

iPhone 15 Pro Overview

The iPhone 15 Pro is Apple's flagship smartphone, filled with cutting-edge features and technology. In this section, we'll present a summary of what distinguishes the iPhone 15 Pro:

Design Excellence: The stainless-steel frame and ceramic shield front cover on the iPhone 15 Pro give it a premium appearance. Its sleek and robust design not only looks gorgeous but also gives superb protection.

Stunning Super Retina XDR Display: The gadget boasts a Super Retina XDR OLED display with ProMotion technology. It boasts brilliant colors, deep blacks, and a buttery-smooth 120Hz refresh rate, giving a visually engaging experience.

Pro Camera System: The iPhone 15 Pro's camera system is a photographer's dream. It has a triple-lens system with ultra-wide, wide, and telephoto lenses. Features like Night mode, Deep Fusion, and Smart HDR make it very adaptable, assuring great picture and video quality.

ProRAW and ProRes Video: For photography and videography enthusiasts, the iPhone 15 Pro supports ProRAW for high-quality picture editing and ProRes video recording for cinematic video capture.

A15 Bionic Chip: This powerhouse of a chip provides lightning-fast performance and efficient multitasking. Your applications function efficiently, and games and AR experiences are very engaging.

5G Connectivity: With 5G support, you'll experience quicker download and upload speeds, making streaming, video chats, and online gaming smoother than before.

Face ID: The iPhone 15 Pro incorporates Face ID for safe and easy identification. Your face is your password, and it works in varied lighting situations.

iOS & App Ecosystem: Apple's iOS delivers a smooth user experience with frequent upgrades and access to a huge ecosystem of applications, including productivity tools, entertainment, and creative apps.

Long Battery Life: The iPhone 15 Pro delivers exceptional battery life, and with features like Optimized Battery Charging, it guarantees your battery health is protected over time.

MagSafe Technology: MagSafe compatibility enables the simple connection of numerous accessories, including MagSafe chargers, cases, and wallets, improving your iPhone's utility.

Environmental Initiatives: Apple is devoted to sustainability. The iPhone 15 Pro contains recyclable materials and is developed with energy efficiency in mind.

Privacy and Security: Apple values user privacy and security. Features like App Tracking Transparency and privacy-focused options offer you greater control over your data.

The iPhone 15 Pro is a gadget that excels in design, performance, and photographic skills. Whether you're a passionate photographer, a power user, or just searching for a top-tier smartphone experience, the iPhone 15 Pro is built to fulfill your expectations.

Getting Started

In this part, we'll walk you through the basic setup procedure for your iPhone 15 Pro, helping you get off on the right foot.

Unboxing and Contents:

When you unbox your iPhone 15 Pro, you'll discover the smartphone itself, a USB-C to Lightning connector, and a SIM card ejection tool.

Ensure all materials are present and in excellent shape before starting.

SIM Card Installation:

If you have a SIM card, use the provided ejection tool to open the SIM card tray.

Carefully insert your SIM card, ensuring it lines with the tray's notch.

Gently shut the tray and turn on your smartphone.

First-Time Boot:

Press and hold the power button (placed on the right side) until you see the Apple logo.

Follow the on-screen instructions to pick your language, region, and Wi-Fi network.

You can set up your device as fresh or restore from a prior backup using iCloud or iTunes.

Face ID/Touch ID Setup (If applicable): Follow the on-screen steps to set up Face ID or Touch ID for secure authentication.

Apple ID and iCloud: Sign in using your Apple ID or create a new one. Your Apple ID is vital for accessing Apple services and iCloud for backups and data storage.

Privacy and Location Settings: Review and change your privacy and location settings to your taste.

Create or Restore from Backup: You may restore your new iPhone 15 Pro from a previous iCloud or iTunes backup. Alternatively, set it up as a new device.

Screen Time and App Analytics: Choose whether to activate Screen Time and App Analytics for tracking your device use and app performance.

True Tone Display (Optional): You may activate or turn off True Tone to adapt the display's color temperature depending on ambient light conditions.

Choose Light or Dark option: Select your desired look option for the interface - Light or Dark Mode.

Set Up Siri (Optional):

Configure Siri settings and educate your voice assistant for tailored replies.

Once you've finished these first setup procedures, your iPhone 15 Pro will be ready to use.

You may start exploring its features, installing applications, and configuring your smartphone to your preference. The following parts of this book will go further into certain features of your iPhone to help you make the most of its potential.

Unboxing and Setup

When you first unbox your iPhone 15 Pro, it's an exciting moment. This section will help you through the process of unpacking and setting up your new gadget.

Unboxing:

Carefully remove the outer wrapping, taking care not to harm the box within.

Slide off the box's top cover, and you'll discover your iPhone 15 Pro sitting within a protective plastic sleeve.

Contents:

Here's what you should find inside the box:

iPhone 15 Pro

USB-C to Lightning cable

SIM card ejection tool

Documentation (including a Quick Start Guide)

Checking the Contents:

Before starting, confirm that all the goods specified above are present and in excellent shape.

If anything is missing or damaged, contact Apple Support or your merchant.

SIM Card Installation:

If you have a SIM card that you wish to use with your iPhone 15 Pro, follow these steps:

On the right side of your smartphone is where you'll find the SIM card tray.

Use the SIM card ejection tool (or a little paperclip) to push into the small hole in the tray gently. This will release the tray.

Carefully remove the tray.

Place your SIM card in the tray, aligning it with the notched corner.

Slide the tray back into the device until it snaps into place.

First-Time Boot:

Now that your SIM card is in position, it's time to switch up your iPhone 15 Pro for the first time:

Press and hold the power button found on the right side of your smartphone until you see the Apple logo on the screen.

Follow the on-screen directions to pick your language, region, and Wi-Fi network.

Setting Up Your iPhone:

You'll be directed through many setup procedures, including:

Choosing to start up your device as fresh or restore from a previous backup (iCloud or iTunes).

Setting up Face ID or Touch ID for secure authentication.

Signing in using your Apple ID or establishing a new one. Your Apple ID is vital for accessing Apple services, including iCloud for backups.

Reviewing and modifying privacy settings to your taste.

Enabling or disabling True Tone display (adjusts screen color temperature depending on ambient light).

Selecting your desired look mode: Light or Dark Mode.

Configuring Siri settings and training your voice assistant for tailored replies.

Once you've finished these first setup procedures, your iPhone 15 Pro will be ready for usage.

You may begin exploring its features, installing applications, and adjusting settings to suit your interests. This tutorial will further aid you in optimizing your iPhone 15 Pro experience.

SIM Card Installation

If you have a SIM card that you wish to use with your iPhone 15 Pro, follow these instructions to install it:

Locate the SIM Card Tray: The SIM card tray is normally placed on the right side of your iPhone 15 Pro. It's a narrow, rectangular slot with a tiny hole.

Gather Your Tools: You'll need the SIM card ejection tool that came with your iPhone 15 Pro's package. If you don't have it, you may use a little paperclip, but be cautious not to harm the gadget.

Power Off Your iPhone: Before you insert or remove the SIM card, it's a recommended habit to switch off your iPhone. You may accomplish this by pushing and holding the power button until the "slide to power off" slider displays on the screen. Slide it to switch off the gadget.

Insert the Ejection Tool: Take the SIM card ejection tool and insert it into the little hole on the SIM card tray. Apply modest pressure until the tray pops out slightly. If you're using a paperclip, straighten it out and gently slide it into the hole until the tray comes out.

Remove the SIM Card Tray: Carefully take the SIM card tray out of the iPhone. It will fall out easily after you've loosened it. Place the tray on a level surface.

Place the SIM Card: Take your SIM card and check it's correctly positioned. Most SIM cards have a corner that's chopped off or notched. Align this corner with the notch in the tray. Gently insert the SIM card into the tray, ensuring it fits firmly inside the defined space.

Reinsert the SIM Card Tray: Carefully slip the SIM card tray back into the iPhone. It should glide in effortlessly without any resistance. Ensure that the tray is completely installed and flush with the iPhone's side.

Power On Your iPhone: Holding down the power button will cause the Apple logo to appear on the screen. Your iPhone will start up.

SIM Activation: Your iPhone will identify the SIM card and try to activate it. Follow any on-screen instructions to finish the activation procedure.

Once the activation is complete, your iPhone 15 Pro is available to use with your SIM card. You should now be able to make calls, send messages, and access mobile data via your carrier's network.

First-Time Boot

When you switch up your iPhone 15 Pro for the first time, you'll need to go through some basic setup procedures to make your smartphone ready for usage. Here's how to do it:

Power On Your iPhone: To turn on your iPhone 15 Pro, find the power button. On the iPhone 15 Pro, the power button is normally situated on the right side of the smartphone. Press and hold the power button until you see the Apple logo on the screen. This means that your gadget is starting up.

Language and Region Selection: After the Apple logo displays, you'll be welcomed with the "Hello" screen. Follow the on-screen prompts to pick your desired language and location. This decision controls the language your iPhone will use and the regional settings.

Wi-Fi Network: Next, you'll need to connect your iPhone to a Wi-Fi network. From the available options, pick your network, then enter your Wi-Fi password if necessary. A Wi-Fi connection is necessary for finishing the setup procedure and using online services.

Quick Start or Set Up Manually: You'll have two choices for setting up your iPhone:

Quick Start: You can utilize Quick Start to wirelessly transfer your data, Apple ID, and settings to your new iPhone if you have another iOS device running iOS 11 or later. Follow the on-screen directions and bring your previous smartphone near your new iPhone to commence the transfer.

Set Up Manually: If you don't have another iOS device or want to set up your iPhone manually, you may pick this option. You'll need to input your Apple ID and other credentials step by step.

Face ID/Touch ID Setup (If applicable): If your iPhone 15 Pro supports Face ID or Touch ID, you'll be required to set up this feature for secure authentication. To register your face or fingerprint, adhere to the on-screen instructions.

Apple ID Sign-In: Sign in with your current Apple ID or create a new one. Your Apple ID is crucial for accessing the App Store, iCloud, and other Apple services. If you don't have an Apple ID, you may create one at this stage.

Data & Privacy: Review and change your privacy settings. Apple provides you control over how your data is used and shared. Adjust these options according to your preferences.

Restore from iCloud/iTunes Backup (Optional): If you have a prior iPhone backup saved in iCloud or iTunes, you may opt to restore your new iPhone from that backup. This will move your applications, settings, and data to your new smartphone. If you choose to start anew, click "Set Up as New iPhone."

Screen Time and App statistics: Decide whether you wish to activate Screen Time and share app statistics with Apple. These options let you monitor your device consumption and optimize app performance, respectively.

True Tone Display (Optional): You may activate or disable True Tone during this setup. True Tone changes the display's color temperature depending on ambient light for a more pleasant viewing experience.

Light or Dark Mode: Choose your favorite appearance mode: Light or Dark Mode. You may always alter this later in Settings.

Siri Setup (Optional): Configure Siri settings, including voice activation and voice feedback choices.

Once you've finished these setup procedures, your iPhone 15 Pro will be ready to use. You may start exploring its features, installing applications, and configuring your smartphone to your preference.

Navigating Your iPhone

Navigating your iPhone 15 Pro is a crucial component of utilizing it efficiently. Here's a basic description of how to browse your device:

Home Screen Basics: Your home screen is the primary interface of your iPhone. It shows app icons, widgets, and a dock at the bottom. To return to the home screen from any app or screen, swipe up from the bottom of the screen (gesture-based navigation) or click the home button (if present).

Control Center: Swipe down from the top right of the screen (or swipe up from the bottom edge on certain models) to open the Control Center. Control Center enables easy access to critical settings, including Wi-Fi, Bluetooth, screen brightness, and more.

Notification Center: Swipe down from the top center or top left corner of the screen to reach the Notification Center. Here, you'll discover alerts, widgets, and the Today View with information like your calendar events and weather.

App Library: To reach the App Library, slide left from your previous home screen page. The App Library automatically organizes your applications into categories, making it simple to discover and activate them.

App Switcher (Multitasking): To switch between previously used applications, slide up from the bottom of the screen and hold for a second. This will launch the App Switcher. Swipe left or right to navigate between the open applications, then press one to switch to it.

Siri (Voice Assistant): Activate Siri by saying "Hey Siri" (if enabled) or by pushing and holding the side button (power button). You may ask Siri questions, make reminders, send messages, and conduct numerous operations using voice commands.

Spotlight Search: To see the search bar, swipe down on the home screen. This is Spotlight Search. Use it to swiftly discover programs, contacts, emails, and more on your smartphone.

Gestures: The iPhone 15 Pro depends on gestures for navigation. Learn typical movements like swiping, pinching, and tapping to interact with applications and information.

Control Center Shortcuts: Customize Control Center shortcuts by heading to Settings > Control Center. You may add or delete shortcuts for fast access to your most-used functions.

Multitasking Gestures (If supported): On certain iPhone models, you may utilize multitasking gestures. For example, swipe left or right on the bottom edge of the screen to move between open applications.

iPhone 15 Pro Phone Guide

Navigating your iPhone 15 Pro is straightforward and made to be efficient. With experience, you'll grow accustomed to these gestures and capabilities, making it easier to access and operate the different tasks of your smartphone.

Home Screen Basics

Your iPhone 15 Pro's home screen is your major hub for accessing applications and information. Here are the fundamentals of how to access and utilize your iPhone's home screen:

Unlocking Your iPhone: To unlock your iPhone, just hit the power button (found on the right side) or use Face ID (if set). If you're using Touch ID, rest your finger on the Home button.

Locating Apps: App icons are presented on the home screen. Tap an icon to access the related app. Swipe left or right to browse between several home screen pages. You may have numerous pages packed with applications.

App Folders: Apps may be arranged into folders to keep your home screen neat. To build a folder, press and hold an app until it begins jiggling, then drag it onto another app. This will create a folder containing both programs. To open a folder, touch on it. To close it, hit the home button or swipe down on the screen (on devices with gesture-based navigation).

The Dock: At the bottom of the home screen is a row of app icons called the dock. It enables easy access to your most-used applications. You may edit the applications in the dock by touching and holding an app icon and then dragging it to the dock.

Widgets (iOS 14 and later): Widgets give at-a-glance information and simple actions. To add widgets, slide left to the Today View or the far left home screen page, then press "Edit" at the bottom. Tap the "+" button to add widgets and change their size and placement.

App Library (iOS 14 and later): Swipe left from your last home screen page to reach the App Library, which automatically organizes your applications into categories. You may search for applications in the App Library or touch on a category to view all apps within it.

Search: Swipe down from the center of the home screen to access the search bar (Spotlight Search). Here, you may search for applications, contacts, messages, and more on your smartphone.

Customization: You may personalize your home screen by rearranging app icons, adding folders, and changing backgrounds. To accomplish this, press and hold an app icon until it begins jiggling, then drag it to a new place or onto another app to form a folder.

App Deletion: To remove an app from your home screen, press and hold an app icon until it jiggles, then hit the "X" button that appears in the corner of the app's icon. Confirm the deletion if requested.

Control Center: Swipe down from the top right corner of the screen to open Control Center, which allows easy access to settings and features, including Wi-Fi, Bluetooth, and screen brightness.

The home screen is where you'll spend most of your time on your iPhone, so feel free to modify it to fit your tastes and keep your most-used applications within easy reach.

Control Center

Control Center is a helpful feature on your iPhone 15 Pro that allows fast access to critical settings and tasks. You can access the Control Center from anywhere on your smartphone, making it simple to alter numerous settings on the move. Here's how to utilize Control Center effectively:

Accessing Control Center: To access Control Center, swipe up from the bottom edge of some models or down from the upper right corner of the screen, depending on your iOS version and preferences. When you scroll down, the Control Center menu will display, allowing you rapid access to numerous functions and shortcuts.

Control Center Components: The Control Center is organized into numerous parts, each offering access to certain functions:

Top area: The top area of the Control Center shows crucial information such as the time, date, battery %, and any scheduled appointments from your calendar.

Connectivity and Music Controls: Just below the top section, you'll find controls for Wi-Fi, Bluetooth, Cellular Data, Airplane Mode, and music playing. You may turn these settings on or off with a single press.

Brightness and Volume Controls: Sliders for changing screen brightness and volume are situated in the center of the Control Center. You may swipe left or right on these sliders to modify the levels.

Toggles and Shortcuts: The bottom half of the Control Center provides numerous toggles and shortcuts for widely used features, including Do Not Disturb, Screen Rotation Lock, Silent Mode, and more. Tap these icons to activate or disable the corresponding functionalities.

Music and Media Playback: If you're playing music or media on your device, playback controls will show in the Control Center. You may play, stop, skip songs, and control the volume here.

Customizing Control Center: You may configure the Control Center to add or delete particular controls depending on your preferences.

To accomplish this:

Go to "Settings" on your iPhone.

Scroll down and pick "Control Center."

Here, you may add or delete controls by touching the "+" or "-" buttons next to each choice.

Additional Control Center tools: The Control Center also enables easy access to devices like the flashlight, calculator, camera, and more, depending on your settings and app availability.

Control Center is a sophisticated tool for controlling your device's settings and operations with ease. Whether you want to change screen brightness, activate Wi-Fi, or manage your music playing, it's only a swipe away for fast and effortless access.

Notification Center

Notification Center is a critical feature on your iPhone 15 Pro that keeps you updated about important updates, messages, and events. It gives a consolidated spot for organizing and seeing alerts from numerous applications. Here's how to utilize the Notification Center effectively:

Accessing Notification Center: To launch Notification Center, swipe down from the top center or top left corner of your iPhone's screen. You may do this from the lock screen or while using your smartphone.

Notification Center Components:

Notification Center is separated into many categories to help you handle your alerts efficiently:

Today View: The top portion of the Notification Center is called the "Today View." Here, you may view widgets that give at-a-glance information, such as your upcoming calendar events, weather, and news headlines. You may edit the widgets that are displayed in the Today View by pressing "Edit" at the bottom of this section.

Notification Cards: Below the Today View, you'll discover a collection of notification cards. Each card represents a notification from a single app. Notifications are categorized by app, making it more straightforward to detect and handle them. To engage with a notice, touch on it. This will launch the related app or present alternatives for reacting to the notice, depending on the app's capabilities.

Clearing Notifications: To clear a single notification, slide it to the left or right, then press "Clear" or "View" (depending on the app). To delete all notifications, touch "delete All" at the top of the notification cards area. This will erase all alerts from the Notification Center.

Customizing Notification Settings:

You may modify how alerts are presented and handled on your iPhone:

App-Specific Settings: Go to "Settings" > "Notifications" to access app-specific notification settings. Here, you may customize the sorts of alerts each app can deliver, including banners, noises, and badges.

Notification Grouping: iOS automatically organizes alerts by app. You may opt to keep alerts grouped or have them shown separately. To alter this option, go to "Settings" > "Notifications" > "Notification Grouping."

Do Not Disturb: Use Do Not Disturb mode to quiet alerts momentarily. You may adjust when and how this mode is triggered under "Settings" > "Do Not Disturb."

Scheduled Summary (iOS 15 and later): Scheduled Summary enables you to get alerts in a batch at preset times to prevent distractions. You may set up a Scheduled Summary under "Settings" > "Notifications."

Notification Center is a useful tool for keeping organized and informed. By controlling your notifications properly and personalizing your settings, you can guarantee that your iPhone 15 Pro functions effortlessly to keep you informed without overloading you with continual alerts.

App Library

You can use the App Library on your iPhone 15 Pro. It was added in iOS 14. It automatically arranges your applications into categories, making it more straightforward to discover and access them without cluttering your home screen. Here's how to utilize the App Library effectively:

Accessing the App Library:

Go to your last home screen page (swipe left from the home screen). You'll now be in the App Library view.

App Library Components:

The App Library is grouped into numerous categories, and it gives a quick method to search and access your apps:

Categories: Apps are sorted into categories like "Recently Added," "Utilities," "Social," and more. These categories are automatically formed based on the kind and use of the applications.

Suggestions: The top row of the App Library offers recommended applications depending on your use habits and the time of day. These recommendations vary constantly to enable rapid access to relevant applications.

Alphabetical List: Below the recommended applications, You'll see an alphabetical listing of all the apps you've installed. You may swipe down on this list to show an alphabetical grid for speedier app access.

Search: At the top of the App Library, there's a search box. You may use this bar to search for a certain app by name.

Using the App Library:

Touch to launch: To launch an app from the App Library, touch its icon. The App Library will shut, and the chosen app will open.

Search: Use the search box at the top to quickly discover an app by inputting its name.

Categories: Explore the many types to find applications depending on their nature and purpose. You may touch on a variety to view all the applications inside it.

Remove Apps from Home Screen: If you wish to simplify your home screen by eliminating app icons, you may do so without uninstalling the apps. Tap and hold an app on your home screen until it enters the "jiggly" mode. Then, to delete the program from the home screen, click the small "x" symbol on its icon. The App Library will continue to provide the app.

Customization: To further configure the App Library, you may click on "Settings" > "Home Screen" and pick how you want newly downloaded applications to be displayed: on the home screen, in the App Library exclusively, or both.

The App Library is meant to ease app administration and eliminate home screen clutter. It's particularly beneficial if you have several applications loaded and want a more structured and effective method to access them.

Touch and Gestures

Your iPhone 15 Pro depends on touch and gestures for navigation and interaction. Understanding these touch and gesture capabilities is vital for operating your smartphone efficiently. Here's a tutorial on some typical touch and gestures you'll use on your iPhone:

Tap: A simple tap is a basic motion. You press an app icon to launch it. To follow a link, tap on it, or To write, press the keys on the keyboard.

Double Tap: Some programs and services allow for double-tapping. For instance, double-tap the screen while viewing a video to zoom in or out.

Long Press (Press and Hold): Press and hold your finger on an app icon, link, or other components to initiate extra actions. This motion may display choices like renaming programs, relocating them, or uninstalling them.

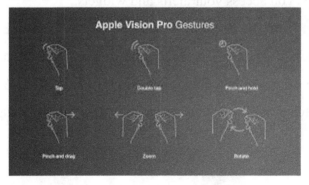

Swipe:

Swipe Left or Right: Swipe your finger left or right across the screen to navigate between lists, pages, or photographs horizontally.

Swipe Up or Down: Swipe up or down to navigate across material vertically. This motion is often used in online surfing, social networking, and reading articles.

Pinch: To zoom in or out on an image, map, or website, use two fingers on the screen. To zoom in or out, spread them apart or pinch them together.

Spread: The reverse of pinch, spreading your fingers apart on the screen enlarges the stuff you're seeing, such as a picture or a webpage.

Rotation: To change the orientation of your screen (portrait to landscape or vice versa), rotate your smartphone. Auto-rotation is normally allowed by default; however, you may lock it in portrait mode through the Control Center if desired.

Swipe Down from the Top: This motion-activated Notification Center lets you access your alerts and widgets.

Swipe Up from the Bottom: Swipe Up from the Bottom Edge: This gesture returns you to the home screen, removing the need for a hardware home button. Swipe Up Slightly and Hold: Access the App Switcher to switch between previously used applications.

Swipe Down from the Right Corner: This gesture activates the Control Center, offering fast access to settings and functionalities, including Wi-Fi, Bluetooth, and screen brightness.

Three-Finger Touch (Accessibility): In the Accessibility settings, you may allow a three-finger touch to initiate specific capabilities, such as magnification or VoiceOver.

Shake: Some programs and features employ a shaking gesture to initiate actions like undoing or redoing text input.

Force Touch (If Supported): On devices that allow it, applying varied amounts of pressure to the screen may trigger extra functionalities or shortcuts, such as "Peek and Pop" for previewing material.

These are some of the primary touch and gesture controls you'll use on your iPhone 15 Pro. The particular motions might change significantly based on your iOS version and individual program interactions. Exploring these gestures and becoming used to them can improve your overall iPhone experience and simplify your interactions with your device.

Multi-Touch Gestures

Your iPhone 15 Pro supports a number of multi-touch gestures that allow you to engage with your smartphone in more natural and efficient ways. These gestures enable you to conduct numerous operations and manage your iPhone with ease. Here are some of the important multi-touch gestures:

Pinch to Zoom:

Place two fingers on the screen (usually on an image, website, or map).

Pinch your fingers together to zoom out.

Spread your fingers apart to zoom in.

Tap and Hold (Long Press):

To view more options or actions, tap and hold your finger on an object or app icon.

For example, You can reorganize or remove apps in "jiggle mode," which you can get by simply tapping the home screen icon of an app.

Two-Finger Scroll:

When reading material that needs scrolling, including websites or documents, use two fingers to scroll.

Swipe up with two fingers to scroll down, and swipe down with two fingers to scroll up.

Swipe:

Swipe Left or Right: Swipe left or right across the screen to browse between pages, images, or items in lists.

Swipe Up or Down: Swipe up or down to browse through material, such as emails, messages, or social network feeds.

Rotation:

When viewing material in landscape mode (horizontal), you may spin your smartphone to convert to portrait mode (vertical) and vice versa.

Auto-rotation may be activated or disabled in the Control Center.

Three-Finger Tap (Accessibility): In the Accessibility settings, you may activate a three-finger tap gesture to initiate different functionalities like magnification or VoiceOver.

Three-Finger Swipe (Accessibility): In Accessibility settings, you may activate a three-finger swipe motion to browse between open applications or use the App Switcher.

Shake: Some programs and functionalities employ a shaking motion as a gesture to activate actions like undoing or redoing text input.

Pinch and Spread with Three Fingers (Accessibility): In Accessibility settings, you may allow this motion to zoom in and out across the full screen.

Three-Finger motions for Cut, Copy, and Paste (Accessibility): In Accessibility settings, you may allow three-finger motions to do activities like cut, copy, and paste.

Two-Finger Touch: In certain applications, a two-finger touch may be utilized for specialized operations, such as zooming in maps or cycling between keyboard languages.

Force Touch (If Supported): On devices that allow it, applying varied amounts of pressure to the screen may trigger extra functionalities or shortcuts, such as "Peek and Pop" for previewing material.

These multi-touch motions make your iPhone experience more intuitive and responsive. Familiarizing yourself with these motions will help you manage your iPhone 15 Pro effectively and take full benefit of its possibilities.

Haptic Touch (If applicable)

Haptic touch is a feature featured on various iPhone models, notably the iPhone 15 Pro. It delivers tactile input (haptic feedback) when you press and hold on the screen, allowing rapid access to additional activities and information. Here's how to utilize Haptic Touch effectively:

Accessing Haptic Touch:

Press and Hold: To enable Haptic Touch, press and hold your finger on an app icon, a link, or a notification banner. The length of the press should be somewhat longer than a conventional tap but less than a "3D Touch" (if your device allows it).

Actions using Haptic Touch:

Depending on where you utilize Haptic Touch, you may access numerous activities and shortcuts:

App Icons: On app icons, Haptic Touch provides a fast actions menu with shortcuts to popular app operations. For example, on the Camera app icon, you may access features like shooting a selfie or making a video immediately from the home screen.

Links and Webpages: When you Haptic Touch a link or a website preview in Safari or other applications, it may provide choices to open the link, add it to your reading list, or copy it.

Notification Banners: When a notification banner displays at the top of the screen, Haptic Touch enables you to expand the notice to read additional information or interact with it. For example, with a messaging notice, you may expand it to see and react to the message without leaving your current app.

Control Center: In the Control Center, Haptic Touch on specific icons or controls gives extra settings or choices. For instance, Haptic Touch the Wi-Fi symbol to access available Wi-Fi networks or the music playing controls for additional possibilities.

Customizing Haptic Touch:

You may change Haptic Touch settings to suit your preferences:

Activate/Disable Haptic Touch: To activate or disable Haptic Touch, go to "Settings" > "Accessibility" > "Touch," and turn on or off the "Haptic Touch" option.

Haptic Touch Sensitivity: You may modify the sensitivity of Haptic Touch by heading to "Settings" > "Accessibility" > "Touch" > "Haptic Touch" and selecting between "Light," "Medium," or "Firm" touch durations.

Haptic touch improves the user experience on your iPhone 15 Pro by enabling rapid access to tasks and shortcuts. By utilizing it properly, you may save time and simplify your interactions with applications and alerts.

Making Calls and Texting

Your iPhone 15 Pro enables you to make calls and send text messages quickly. Here's how to utilize these crucial communication features:

Making Calls:

Dial a Number:

Open the Phone app from the home screen.

Tap the keypad symbol at the bottom.

Enter the phone number you wish to call.

Tap the green "Call" button to begin the call.

Call Contacts:

Open the Phone app.

Tap the "Contacts" tab at the bottom.

Scroll or search for the contact you wish to call.

Tap the contact's name.

Tap the green "Call" button.

Recent Calls:

Open the Phone app.

Tap the "Recents" tab at the bottom.

Tap a recent call to redial it.

Favorites:

Open the Phone app.

Tap the "Favorites" option at the bottom.

Add frequently called contacts to your favorites list for easy access.

Voicemail: To check voicemail, open the Phone app and hit the "Voicemail" option at the bottom. Sending Text Messages (iMessage/SMS):

Messages App:

Open the Messages app from the home screen.

Tap the compose button (typically a pencil symbol) in the upper-right corner.

In the "To:" area, put the recipient's name or phone number.

Type your message in the text area at the bottom.

Tap the blue send button (typically a paper aircraft symbol) to send your message.

Group Messages: You may send group messages by specifying numerous recipients in the "To:" column.

iMessage vs. SMS: iMessage is used for sending messages to other iOS devices and Macs via the Internet. It's shown with blue bubbles. SMS (Short Message Service) is used for sending messages to non-Apple devices. Green bubbles show it.

Attachments: You may transmit photographs, videos, documents, and more by pressing the camera icon next to the text area.

Emojis and Stickers: Tap the happy face symbol to access emojis and stickers to add fun and personality to your communications.

Voice Messages: To record and transmit a voicemail, long-press the microphone icon.

Tapback Reactions: You may respond to a message with a tapback by pressing and holding a message and picking a response like a thumbs-up or a heart.

Remember to verify your smartphone has a cellular or Wi-Fi connection for calling and messaging. Additionally, your iPhone offers a range of calling and texting services, including FaceTime for video conversations and third-party messaging applications for alternate messaging alternatives. Explore these features to communicate in the style that fits you best.

Making Calls

To make calls on your iPhone 15 Pro, you may utilize the Phone app or voice instructions using Siri. Here's how to make calls using the Phone app:

Using the Phone App:

Open the Phone App: Locate and press the Phone app icon on your home screen. It looks like a green phone receiver.

Dial a Number: Once the Phone app is open, hit the keypad icon at the bottom to access the numeric keypad.

Enter the Phone Number: Use the keyboard to enter the phone number you wish to call.

Initiate the Call: After inputting the number, hit the green "Call" button. Your call will be dialed, and you'll see the call screen with choices to mute, switch to speakerphone, or add another call.

Call from Contacts: If you want to call someone from your contacts, press the "Contacts" option at the bottom of the Phone app, identify the person you want to call and tap their name. Then, hit the green "Call" button.

Using Siri:

Activate Siri: You may also use Siri to make calls hands-free. To activate Siri, either say "Hey Siri" (if it's enabled) or press and hold the side button (power button) until Siri appears.

Call a Contact: You may say something like "Call [Contact Name]" or "Call [Contact's Phone Number]." Siri will confirm and begin the call.

Call a Business: You may ask Siri to call a business by saying, for example, "Call the closest pizza establishment" or "Call [Business Name]."

Call a Number: Say "Call [Phone Number]" to have Siri call the number for you.

Using Favorites: In the Phone app, you may add people you call a lot to your Favorites list. Then, you may instantly access and call them from the Favorites menu.

Using Recent Calls: The Phone app also retains a record of recent calls. You may launch the app, navigate to the "Recents" page, and press a recent call to call that person back.

Remember to check that your iPhone has a cellular connection or is linked to Wi-Fi for making calls. You may also utilize extra capabilities like FaceTime for video calls or third-party communication applications like WhatsApp or Skype for alternate methods to make calls.

Sending Texts and iMessages

You may send both regular SMS text messages and iMessages on your iPhone 15 Pro. iMessages are transmitted via the Internet to other Apple devices and are denoted by blue bubbles. In contrast, SMS messages are delivered over the cellular network to non-Apple devices and are shown by green bubbles. Here's how to send both sorts of messages:

Sending an iMessage:

Open the Messages App: Locate and touch the Messages app icon on your home screen. It looks like a blue conversation bubble.

Compose a New Message: Tap the compose button, normally located in the upper-right corner (it looks like a pencil or a square with a pencil symbol).

Enter the Recipient: In the "To:" section, start entering the name, email, or phone number of the person you wish to communicate. As you write, your contacts will show as recommendations. Tap the contact you wish to message.

Compose Your Message: In the text field located at the bottom of the screen, type your message. You may also hit the microphone symbol to send a voice message or use the camera icon to send photographs or videos.

Send the iMessage: Tap the blue send button (typically a paper aircraft symbol) to send your iMessage.

Sending a Traditional SMS Text Message:

Launch the Messages App: Follow the same steps as previously to launch the Messages app.

Compose a New Message: Tap the compose button (pencil icon) in the upper-right corner.

Enter the Recipient: In the "To:" section, insert the recipient's phone number. You'll see that the message bubble color changes to green, suggesting that this is a regular SMS message.

Compose Your Message: In the text field, type your message as you would in an iMessage.

Send the SMS Message: Tap the blue send button (typically a paper aircraft symbol) to send your SMS message.

Additional Messaging Features:

Group Messages: To send a message to several recipients, add extra names or phone numbers to the "To:" column.

Emojis and Stickers: You may press the smiling face symbol to get a large selection of stickers and emojis to spice up your chats.

Voice Messages: To record and send a voice message, hold down the microphone icon.

Tapback Reactions: You may respond to a received message with a tapback. Press and hold a message, then pick a response like a thumbs-up or a heart.

Message Effects: You may add extra effects to your messages by pressing the "App Store" button next to the text field and exploring several possibilities.

Read Receipts: You may activate or disable read receipts (indicating when you've read a message) under your message settings.

Remember that iMessages need an internet connection, whereas standard SMS texts depend on cellular coverage. Your iPhone automatically decides the sort of message to send depending on the recipient's device and the availability of internet access.

Managing Contacts

Managing contacts on your iPhone is vital for keeping your address book tidy and readily accessible. Here's how to handle your contacts effectively:

Adding Contacts:

Manually Add a Contact:

Open the Contacts app on your iPhone (the symbol resembles a blue silhouette of a person).

Tap the "+" symbol in the top-right corner to add a new contact.

Fill in the contact's name, phone number, email address, and other data.

Tap "Add" to store the contact.

Import Contacts: If you have contacts saved in another account (e.g., Google, Outlook, or iCloud), you may import them to your iPhone. Go to "Settings" > "Contacts" > "Accounts," choose your account, and activate Contacts syncing.

Editing and Updating Contacts: To edit an existing contact, launch the Contacts app, pick the contact you want to modify, and touch on their name. Then, touch "Edit" in the top-right area to make adjustments.

Deleting Contacts: To delete a contact, open the Contacts app, pick the contact you want to remove, press on their name, scroll down, and tap "Delete Contact." Confirm the deletion when asked.

Grouping Contacts: You may arrange your contacts into groups or labels for better access. Open the Contacts app in order to create a contact group, press "Groups" in the top-left corner, then create a new group. Then, assign contacts to appropriate groups.

Backing Up Contacts: To guarantee you don't lose your contacts, it's necessary to back them up often. You may accomplish this with iCloud or other cloud services. Go to "Settings" > "Apple ID" > "iCloud," and verify "Contacts" is enabled to sync your contacts with iCloud.

Merging Duplicate Contacts: Over time, you may amass duplicate contacts. You may combine them to keep your address book neat. Open the Contacts app, choose a contact, hit "Edit," scroll down, and tap "Link Contacts." Then, select the contacts you wish to merge.

Exporting Contacts: If you need to export your contacts, you may do it through iCloud or by utilizing third-party applications. iCloud enables you to export a VCF (vCard) file containing all your contacts. Alternatively, there are applications available on the App Store that give more sophisticated contact export capabilities.

Sharing Contacts: You may quickly share a contact with someone else. Open the Contacts app, choose the contact, press "Share Contact," and choose your preferred method (e.g., message, email, or AirDrop).

Searching Contacts: If you have a big list of contacts, use the search box at the top of the Contacts app to quickly identify a particular contact by name, phone number, or email address.

Contact Settings: Customize contact settings by heading to "Settings" > "Contacts." Here, you may modify contact sorting, display order, and default account settings.

By successfully managing your contacts on your iPhone 15 Pro, you can guarantee that your address book is organized and up to date, making it more straightforward to stay connected with friends, family, and coworkers.

Voicemail

Voicemail is a helpful tool that enables callers to leave you voice messages while you're unable to answer your phone. On your iPhone 15 Pro, voicemail is straightforward to set up and maintain. Here's how to utilize voicemail effectively:

Setting Up Voicemail: When you initially activate your iPhone, the voicemail setting procedure happens typically automatically.

If not, you may set up voicemail manually:

Open the Phone app (the green symbol with a phone receiver).

Tap the "Voicemail" tab at the bottom.

If asked, follow the on-screen directions to set up your voicemail by setting a voicemail password and recording a customized greeting.

Accessing Voicemail: To access your voicemail, open the Phone app and hit the "Voicemail" option at the bottom. This will show a list of your voicemail messages.

Listening to Voicemail: Tap on a voicemail message to listen to it. You may use the on-screen controls to play, stop, rewind, or fast-forward through the message.

Deleting Voicemail: After listening to a voicemail, you may remove it by hitting the "remove" or "Trash" icon. Alternatively, swipe left on the voicemail and press "Delete."

Saving Voicemail: If you wish to preserve a voicemail message for future reference, you may save it by clicking the "Save" or "Preserve" option.

Replying to Voicemail: To respond to a voicemail message with a call, touch the "Call Back" option while listening to the message.

Sharing Voicemail: You may share a voicemail message with others by pressing the "Share" button. This enables you to transmit the voicemail as an audio file using several communication options.

Customizing Voicemail Greeting: To alter your voicemail greeting, open the Phone app, select the "Voicemail" tab, and tap "Greeting" in the upper-left corner. You may record a fresh welcome or pick a pre-recorded one.

Visual voicemail: iPhones feature Visual Voicemail, which shows a list of your voicemail messages with caller data and timestamps. You may pick which messages to listen to without going through them consecutively.

Voicemail Transcription (iOS 10 and later): Voicemail transcription automatically transforms spoken words in a voicemail into text, making it more straightforward to read voicemail messages. You may activate or turn off this function in the Phone app settings.

Please note that voicemail functionality and settings may vary significantly based on your carrier and iOS version. Make sure your iPhone has a cellular or Wi-Fi connection to view voicemail. Voicemail is a helpful tool for handling missed calls and keeping in touch with your contacts when you can't answer your phone.

Internet and Connectivity

Your iPhone 15 Pro provides several methods to access the Internet and remain connected. Here's an overview of internet and connection options:

Cellular Data: Your iPhone enables cellular data connection, enabling you to access the Internet through your mobile carrier's network. Make sure your cellular data is switched on in "Settings" > "Cellular" to utilize this function.

Wi-Fi: Wi-Fi is a popular and quick method to connect to the Internet when you're within range of a wireless network.

To connect to Wi-Fi:

Open the "Settings" app.

Tap "Wi-Fi."

From the list, pick a network, and if necessary, enter the password.

Personal Hotspot: Sharing an internet connection with other devices is possible if you have a cellular data plan, such as laptops or tablets, by turning your iPhone into a personal hotspot. To set up a personal hotspot, go to "Settings" > "Personal Hotspot" and follow the steps.

Bluetooth: Bluetooth enables you to connect your iPhone to other Bluetooth-enabled devices, such as headphones, speakers, keyboards, and more. This is largely for device connection rather than internet access.

VPN (Virtual Private Network): You may establish a VPN on your iPhone to increase online privacy and security. VPNs transport your internet traffic via secure servers, shielding your data from prying eyes.

Airplane Mode: All wireless connections, including Bluetooth, Wi-Fi, and cellular data, are turned off when using Airplane Mode. It's handy while traveling or in circumstances when you need to switch off all connections.

5G and Wi-Fi 6: Depending on your carrier and region, your iPhone 15 Pro may feature 5G cellular connection and Wi-Fi 6 for faster download and upload rates when connected to compatible networks. Network Settings: You can control network settings in the "Settings" app under "Cellular," "Wi-Fi," and "Bluetooth." Here, you can customize network preferences, monitor data use, and connect to recognized networks.

AirDrop: AirDrop enables you to exchange files, photographs, and more with nearby Apple devices through Wi-Fi and Bluetooth. It's an easy method to transmit material rapidly.

Find My iPhone: The "Find My iPhone" function utilizes internet access to help find your handset if it's lost or stolen. You may use this function using the Find My app.

iCloud and Cloud Services: iCloud and other cloud services allow you to sync and access your data, photographs, and documents across different devices, provided you have an internet connection.

App Store and Updates: You may download applications, games, and updates from the App Store through a Wi-Fi or cellular connection.

Your iPhone 15 Pro provides a broad choice of connection options to keep you connected to the Internet, other devices, and online services. Whether you're surfing the web, streaming entertainment, or utilizing applications, these connection capabilities are vital for keeping connected and getting the most out of your smartphone.

Connecting to Wi-Fi

Open Settings: Unlock your iPhone and navigate to the home screen. Locate and touch the "Settings" app. It features a gearwheel symbol and is commonly seen on the home screen.

Access Wi-Fi Settings: In the Settings app, go down and touch "Wi-Fi." You'll reach the Wi-Fi settings panel as a result.

Enable Wi-Fi: If Wi-Fi is presently switched off, press the button at the top of the screen to enable Wi-Fi. It will glow green when activated.

Select a Wi-Fi Network: Under the "Choose a Network..." section, your iPhone will show a list of accessible Wi-Fi networks. Tap the name of the Wi-Fi network you wish to connect to.

Enter the Wi-Fi Password (if required): If the chosen network is password-protected, you will be requested to enter the Wi-Fi password. Type in the correct password using the on-screen keypad, then touch "Join" or "Connect."

Wait for Connection: Your iPhone will try to connect to the specified Wi-Fi network. Once connected, you'll notice a checkmark next to the network name.

Connected to Wi-Fi: You are now connected to the Wi-Fi network, and your iPhone will utilize this connection for internet access.

Auto-Join and Auto-Connect (Optional): If you want your iPhone to automatically connect to this Wi-Fi network whenever it's in range, ensure the "Auto-Join" or "Auto-Connect" option (if applicable) is set for that network.

Forget a Wi-Fi Network (Optional): If you no longer want your iPhone to connect to a specific Wi-Fi network, hit the "i" symbol next to the network name, then tap "Forget This Network."

Wi-Fi Assist (Optional): Under Wi-Fi settings, you'll discover "Wi-Fi Assist." When enabled, When Wi-Fi connectivity is weak, this feature enables your iPhone to switch to a cellular connection automatically.

Wi-Fi Calling (Carrier-Dependent and Optional): If your carrier offers Wi-Fi calling, you may activate it in the "Phone" section of the Settings app. This enables you to make calls via Wi-Fi when your cellular connection is poor.

That's it! You're now connected to Wi-Fi on your iPhone 15 Pro. Wi-Fi is particularly beneficial for quicker internet access, saving cellular data, and connecting to secure networks, such as your home or business Wi-Fi.

Cellular Data

Cellular data enables you to browse the internet and utilize online services while you're away from Wi-Fi networks. Here's how to utilize cellular data on your iPhone 15 Pro:

Enable Cellular Data: By default, your iPhone should have cellular data enabled. You may verify and activate it if required by following these steps:

Open the "Settings" app from your home screen.

Scroll down and hit "Cellular."

Ensure the "Cellular Data" switch is switched on. It should be green when enabled.

Monitor Data consumption: It's crucial to keep an eye on your cellular data consumption, particularly if you have a restricted data plan. You may monitor your consumption and set data limitations by following these steps:

In the "Settings" app, go to "Cellular."

Scroll down to get your data consumption details, including how much data each app has consumed.

Tap "Cellular Data use" to get a list of applications and their data use.

App-Specific Cellular Data Settings: You may choose which applications are authorized to utilize cellular data, helping you manage your data consumption efficiently:

In the "Settings" app, go to "Cellular."

Scroll down to view a list of installed applications.

Toggle the switch next to each app to enable or limit cellular data use for that app.

Roaming (Optional): When going overseas, be wary about data roaming prices. You may activate or disable data roaming in the "Cellular" settings to prevent unexpected expenses.

Reset Cellular Data consumption: If you wish to reset your data consumption statistics to monitor usage for a specified time, go to the bottom of the "Cellular" options and press "Reset Statistics."

Wi-Fi Assist (Optional): Under the "Cellular" options, you'll discover "Wi-Fi Assist." When enabled, this function enables your iPhone to utilize cellular data when your Wi-Fi connection is poor.

Personal Hotspot (Optional): If you wish to share your cellular data connection with other devices (tethering), you may set up a personal hotspot. Go to "Settings" > "Personal Hotspot" to set up this function.

Data Plan Management: Keep track of your cellular data plan and consider upgrading if you often exceed your data allocation to prevent overage penalties.

Wi-Fi Offloading: Your iPhone may automatically switch to Wi-Fi networks when available to preserve cellular data. This helps decrease data use.

Using cellular data on your iPhone 15 Pro gives you the freedom to remain connected when you're not in range of Wi-Fi. Be conscious of your data consumption, limit which applications may utilize cellular data, and be cautious about data roaming while going overseas to get the most out of your mobile data plan.

AirDrop

AirDrop is a useful function that enables you to wirelessly transfer images, videos, documents, and more with adjacent Apple devices. Here's how to utilize AirDrop on your iPhone 15 Pro:

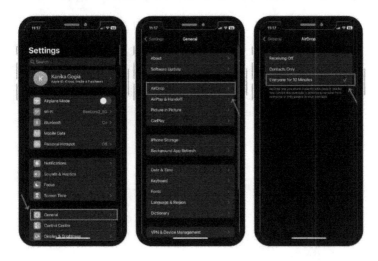

Ensure AirDrop is Enabled: Make sure that AirDrop is enabled on your iPhone. Here's how to verify and enable it:

To open the Control Center, swipe down from the top-right corner of the screen

In the upper-left corner, press and hold the network settings card (it should display your Wi-Fi and cellular connection icons).

In the enlarged card, touch the "AirDrop" symbol.

Choose one of the following options:

Receiving Off: This disables AirDrop.

Contacts Only: Allows only your contacts to send you AirDrop requests.

Everyone: Allows anybody nearby to give you AirDrop requests.

Transmit files using AirDrop: To transmit a file using AirDrop, follow these steps:

Open the app or pick the file you wish to share. This might be a picture, movie, document, or other appropriate asset.

Tap the "Share" button, often depicted by a square with an arrow pointing up. It's frequently found inside the app you're using.

In the sharing choices that display, search for the AirDrop area.

You'll see a list of nearby Apple devices with AirDrop enabled. Tap the device you wish to send the file to.

Accept AirDrop Requests: When someone nearby attempts to give you a file over AirDrop, you'll get an AirDrop request notice. To accept the request, take these steps:

A notice will show on your screen with the sender's name and a preview of the file.

Press "Accept" to get the file, or press "Decline" to reject it.

Receiving AirDrop Files: When you accept an AirDrop request, the file will be immediately stored in the relevant app or directory on your device. For example, photographs will show in your picture's app; papers will move to the Files app, and so on.

Troubleshooting AirDrop: If you find difficulties with AirDrop, such as devices not displaying in the AirDrop menu, attempt the following troubleshooting steps:

Ensure both Wi-Fi and Bluetooth are enabled on your device.

Make sure that the other person's device is within Bluetooth and Wi-Fi range

Check that the recipient's AirDrop settings enable receiving from "Everyone" or "Contacts Only," depending on your desire.

Restart your iPhone if you're encountering persistent AirDrop troubles.

AirDrop is a fast and straightforward method to exchange material with friends, family, or coworkers nearby. It's a convenient tool for sending files without the need for email or chat programs, making it excellent for sharing images, presentations, and more.

Email and Online Services

Your iPhone 15 Pro enables simple access to email and a wide variety of internet services. Here's how to set up and utilize email, as well as access numerous internet services:

Email Setup: To set up an email account on your iPhone 15 Pro:

Open the "Settings" app.

Scroll down and hit "Mail."

Tap "Accounts."

Tap "Add Account" and pick your email provider (e.g., iCloud, Gmail, Yahoo, Outlook, or Other).

Follow the on-screen steps to enter your email address, password, and any other relevant information.

Once established, you may access your email from the "Mail" app on your home screen.

Mail App: With your iPhone, the integrated "Mail" app enables you to send, receive, and manage email from one or many email accounts. You may adjust your email settings, create folders, and arrange your messages.

Online Services: Your iPhone supports a wide variety of online services via applications, including:

Social Media: Access platforms like Facebook, Twitter, Instagram, and LinkedIn through their individual applications or websites.

Cloud Storage: Use iCloud, Google Drive, Dropbox, or other cloud services to store and sync data.

Streaming: Enjoy streaming services like Netflix, Spotify, Apple Music, and YouTube.

Shopping: Shop online using applications like Amazon, eBay, or different retailer-specific apps.

Banking: Manage your funds using mobile banking applications from your bank.

Travel: Access travel services like Airbnb, Expedia, and TripAdvisor for organizing vacations.

News: Stay current with news applications from major news organizations or utilize a news aggregator app.

Communication: Use messaging applications like WhatsApp, Telegram, or Facebook Messenger to communicate with loved ones.

App Store: Your iPhone's App Store is your entrance to hundreds of applications and services. You can browse, download, and install applications to fit your requirements, whether for productivity, entertainment, or remaining connected.

Safari (Web Browser): Use the Safari web browser to access web pages and online services. Bookmark favorite sites, utilize tabs for multitasking, and set reader mode for a distraction-free reading experience.

Password Management: Consider utilizing a password manager tool to securely store and manage your login details for numerous online sites.

Privacy and Security: Be careful of your online privacy and security. Configure your device's privacy settings, activate two-factor authentication for your accounts, and use strong, unique passwords.

App Integration: Many online businesses provide integration with the iOS environment. For example, you may sync your calendar events with Google Calendar or your contacts with your iCloud account.

Updates: Keep your applications and devices updated to ensure you get the latest features and security updates.

Your iPhone 15 Pro has a wide variety of features for accessing and utilizing email and web services. Whether you're writing emails, keeping connected on social media, streaming video, or managing your money, your smartphone delivers a seamless experience for all your online demands.

Setting Up Email Accounts

With the integrated Mail app on your iPhone 15 Pro, setting up and maintaining email accounts is simple. Here's a step-by-step guide to setting up email accounts.

Open the "Settings" App: Unlock your iPhone and proceed to the home screen. Locate and press the "Settings" app icon (it looks like a gearwheel).

Navigate to "Mail": In the Settings app, scroll down and hit "Mail." This will take you to the Mail settings

touch "Accounts": Under the Mail settings, touch "Accounts.

Add Account: Tap "Add Account" to start the email setup procedure.

Choose Your Email Provider: You'll notice a list of popular email providers (e.g., iCloud, Google, Yahoo, Outlook) mentioned. Select your email provider from the list. If your provider isn't mentioned, you may pick "Other" to manually set up your account.

Enter the password and username for your email: Enter your complete email address and password linked with your email account. If you have two-factor authentication set for your email account, you may need to input the verification code received to your trusted device or email.

Sign In or give Access: After entering your email and password, touch "Next" or "Sign In." Follow any on-screen instructions to give the Mail app access to your email account.

Configure Account Settings: Depending on your email provider, the Mail app may automatically configure your email settings. Review and change your account settings as required, such as activating or removing Mail, Contacts, Calendars, and Notes synchronization. You may also choose the number of days of email to sync, manage SSL settings, and more.

Store the Account: After selecting your account settings, touch "Save" or "Done" to store the email account on your iPhone.

Accessing Your Email: Once the account is saved, open the Mail app from your home screen to view your email inbox.

Additional Accounts: If you have several email accounts, you may add them by repeating the previous procedures.

Troubleshooting: If you find any troubles during setup, double-check your email address and password, confirm you have an active internet connection, and validate your email server settings with your email provider.

Your iPhone will now collect emails from your specified accounts, enabling you to view, send, and manage your messages from the Mail app. You may browse your email accounts separately or see them all in one unified inbox, depending on your desire and preferences.

Browsing the Web

Your iPhone 15 Pro comes loaded with Safari, a sophisticated web browser that lets you explore the internet, visit websites, and search for information. Here's how to access the web on your iPhone:

Launch Safari: Locate the Safari icon on your home screen, which looks like a blue compass. Tap it to launch the Safari web browser.

Navigating Web Pages: Use these popular gestures and movements to explore web pages:

Swipe: Swipe up or down to browse across the website.

Pinch and Zoom: Two fingers can be pinched together to zoom in or apart to zoom out.

Tap Links: Tap on links to access new web pages

Back and Forward: Tap the back and forward arrows at the bottom of the screen to browse between previously viewed pages.

Tabs: Tap the square icon in the lower-right corner to see and manage open tabs. You may open new tabs, dismiss tabs, or switch between them.

Bookmarks: Tap the book symbol at the bottom to view your bookmarks and saved sites.

Searching: To search the web, press the address bar at the top of the screen, and your keyboard will display. Type your search phrase, hit "Go," and Safari will show search results.

Bookmarks and Favorites: You may store websites as bookmarks or add them to your favorites for fast access. To accomplish this, hit the "Share" button (which looks like a square with an arrow going up) and pick "Add Bookmark" or "Add to Favorites."

Private browser (Optional): If you wish to surf privately without recording your browser history or cookies, hit the tab switcher icon (two overlapping squares) and choose "Private" to launch a private browsing window.

Reader Mode: Safari features a "Reader" mode for a more concentrated reading experience. Look for the "Reader" symbol in the URL bar while browsing an article, then touch it to activate Reader mode.

Safari Settings: Customize your browser experience by heading to "Settings" > "Safari." Here, you can modify settings like search engine preference, privacy, and more.

Autofill and Passwords: Safari may save and autofill passwords and credit card information for websites you often visit. You may alter this in the Safari settings under "Passwords."

Sharing and Sharing Extensions: Use the "Share" button to share websites through email, messaging, social media, and more. You may also install sharing extensions for extra sharing possibilities.

Reader View (Optional): When reading articles, you may press the "Reader View" icon in the URL bar to simplify the page for simpler reading.

Downloads (iOS 13 and later): Safari enables you to download files. Tap a download link, and the file will be placed in the Downloads folder under the Files app.

Safari on your iPhone is a versatile web browser that delivers a seamless and user-friendly experience. Whether you're exploring the web, reading articles, or doing research, Safari provides the tools and capabilities to improve your browsing experience.

iCloud Services

iCloud is Apple's cloud-based platform that delivers numerous services to let you save, sync, and retrieve your data across your Apple devices, including your iPhone 15 Pro. Here's a summary of iCloud services and how to utilize them:

iCloud Setup: When you initially set up your iPhone 15 Pro, you'll have the choice to sign in or establish an Apple ID, which is important for utilizing iCloud services. If you missed this during setup, you may sign in or establish an Apple ID later in the "Settings" app under "Apple ID."

iCloud Storage: iCloud gives free storage space; however, you may buy more iCloud storage if required. To manage your iCloud storage and upgrade your plan, go to "Settings" > "[Your Name]" > "iCloud" > "Manage Storage" > "Change Storage Plan."

iCloud Services: Here are the key iCloud services and how to utilize them:

iCloud Backup: Automatically backs up your device's settings, app data, and content to the cloud. To activate or adjust iCloud Backup, go to "Settings" > "[Your Name]" > "iCloud" > "iCloud Backup."

Photographs: Automatically save your pictures and videos in iCloud, making them available on all your devices. Enable iCloud Photos under "Settings" > "[Your Name]" > "iCloud" > "Photos."

Contacts, Calendars, and Reminders: Keeps your contacts, calendar events, and reminders in sync across devices. Enable these settings in "Settings" > "[Your Name]" > "iCloud."

Notes: Keep your notes up to date across all your devices. Enable iCloud Notes in "Settings" > "[Your Name]" > "Notes."

Find Me: Helps you find your device if it's lost or stolen. You may use the Find My app on your iPhone or access it through iCloud.com.

iCloud Drive: Stores your files and documents in the cloud, making them available across devices. You may access iCloud Drive using the Files app on your iPhone.

Mail: If you have a @icloud.com email address, you can access your iCloud email account on your iPhone's Mail app.

Keychain: Securely saves your passwords, payment details, and Wi-Fi credentials. Enable iCloud Keychain in "Settings" > "[Your Name]" > "Passwords & Accounts."

Family Sharing: This lets you share iCloud storage, app purchases, and subscriptions with family members. Set up Family Sharing in "Settings" > "[Your Name]" > "Family Sharing."

Data Management: You may manage your iCloud data by navigating to "Settings" > "[Your Name]" > "iCloud." Here, you can decide which applications and data types are kept in iCloud.

iCloud.com: You may view and manage your iCloud data from a web browser by visiting iCloud.com. iCloud Mail, Find My, Photos, and other services can be accessed by logging in with your Apple ID.

Third-Party App Integration: Many third-party applications and services provide integration with iCloud for synchronizing data. Check the settings of your favorite applications to see whether they allow iCloud synchronization.

iCloud services allow seamless data syncing and backup across your Apple devices, boosting your iPhone 15 Pro's usefulness and guaranteeing that your data is always accessible and up to date.

Camera and Photography

Your iPhone 15 Pro is equipped with a sophisticated camera system that enables you to create great images and movies. Here's how to get the most of your iPhone's camera and photography features:

Accessing the Camera: To access the camera, slide left from the lock screen or home screen or hit the Camera app icon on your home screen.

Camera Modes: Your iPhone has different camera modes, including Photo, Video, Portrait, Panorama, and more. Swipe horizontally on the camera interface to switch between modes.

Taking Photos: To take a picture, point your camera towards the subject, then touch the shutter button (a white circle) on the screen or use the physical volume keys.

Taking Burst images (Optional): For moving subjects or action pictures, press and hold the shutter button to record a burst of images. You may afterward choose the finest photo from the burst.

Live Photos (Optional): Live Photos record a few seconds of video before and after capturing a snapshot. To activate Live Photos, press the symbol at the top of the camera interface that looks like concentric circles.

Portrait Mode: Portrait Mode enables you to capture images with a blurred backdrop (bokeh) for a professional effect. It's perfect for portraiture. Access this option by swiping on it in the camera modes.

Night Mode (Low-Light Photography): Night Mode automatically engages in low-light circumstances. Keep your hands steady, and your iPhone will snap well-exposed, low-light images.

Ultra Wide and Telephoto Lenses: Depending on your iPhone model, you may have ultra-wide and telephoto lenses. Switch between lenses by simply touching the 1x, 2x, or 0.5x symbols on the screen.

Zoom and Pinch Gesture: You can zoom in and out by utilizing pinch motions on the camera interface. To zoom in or out, pinch out or pinch in.

Selfies and Front Camera: To switch to the front camera for selfies, press the camera symbol with the arrows in a circle (typically in the top-right corner).

Editing Photos: After snapping a picture, press the preview thumbnail in the bottom-left corner to see it. Tap "Edit" to access editing options, such as crop, filters, changes, and more.

iCloud Photographs: iCloud Photos effortlessly syncs your photographs and videos across your Apple devices. Enable it under "Settings" > "[Your Name]" > "iCloud" > "Photos."

Third-Party Camera Applications: Explore third-party camera applications on the App Store for extra capabilities and creative alternatives.

Video Recording: Swipe to the video mode to start recording videos. You may choose between video resolutions and frame rates in the camera settings.

ProRAW and ProRes (Pro Models): On iPhone Pro models, you can record photographs in ProRAW format for more thorough post-processing. ProRes video recording is provided for professional video quality.

Use Grid and Guidelines: Enable the grid or guidelines in the camera settings to assist in arranging your images more successfully.

The camera on your iPhone 15 Pro is a versatile tool that can meet a range of photographic needs. Whether you're capturing daily moments, exploring creative photography, or shooting in demanding settings, your iPhone's camera hardware and software capabilities equip you with the tools needed to produce outstanding photographs and videos.

Camera App Basics

Accessing the Camera: Swipe left from the lock screen or home screen or hit the Camera app icon to access the Camera app.

Camera Modes: The Camera app has numerous modes, accessible by swiping horizontally on the camera interface. Common modes include:

Picture: Standard picture mode.

Video: Video recording mode.

Portrait: For shooting images with a blurred backdrop (bokeh).

Panorama: To generate broad, sweeping images.

Night Mode: Automatically activates in low-light circumstances.

Square: For square-format photographs, great for social networking.

Time-Lapse: Captures a sequence of photographs over time to produce a time-lapse movie.

Slo-Mo: Records video in slow motion.

Pro (Pro Models): Offers manual control over camera parameters, including ISO, shutter speed, and focus.

Macro (Pro Models): For extreme close-up pictures.

Shutter Button: Tap the white shutter button (circle) on the screen or use the physical volume buttons to snap a shot. For burst photographs, press and hold the shutter button.

Zoom & Lenses: On iPhones with several lenses (ultra-wide, wide, telephoto), you can switch between lenses by touching the 1x, 2x, or 0.5x symbols on the screen. Use pinch movements to zoom in and out.

Live Photos (Optional): Enable Live Photos by pressing the icon at the top of the camera interface. Live Photos record a few seconds of video before and after capturing a snapshot.

Exposure and Focus Control: Tap anywhere on the screen to adjust the focus and exposure point manually. You may change the exposure by moving your finger up or down on the screen after tapping.

Portrait Mode: In Portrait mode, your iPhone employs depth-sensing technology to produce a blurred backdrop behind the subject. This setting is perfect for portraiture.

Night Mode: Night Mode automatically activates in low-light circumstances, letting you shoot well-exposed photographs without flash. Keep your iPhone steady throughout the photo for the best results.

Front and back Cameras: Switch between the front and back cameras by touching the camera symbol with the arrows in a circle.

Editing Photos: After snapping a picture, press the thumbnail in the bottom-left corner to see it. Tap "Edit" to access editing options, including crop, filters, changes, and more.

Flash Control: Tap the lightning bolt symbol to access flash settings. You may opt to turn it off, activate auto-flash, or force it on.

Timer: Tap the timer icon to establish a countdown timer before snapping a picture.

Grid and Guidelines: Enable the grid or guidelines in the camera settings to help you arrange your photographs more successfully.

HDR (dynamic solid Range): HDR automatically adjusts exposure for images with strong contrast. It usually on by default, but you may turn it on or off under the camera settings.

Quick view to Photos and Videos: Swipe left to instantly view the latest photo or movie you recorded without leaving the Camera app.

Third-Party Camera Applications: Explore third-party camera applications on the App Store for extra capabilities and creative alternatives.

The Camera app on your iPhone 15 Pro is intended for simplicity and accessibility while delivering additional options for people who desire greater control over their pictures. Experiment with various modes, settings, and approaches to take photographs and films that fit your creative vision.

Taking Photos and Videos

Capturing images and movies on your iPhone 15 Pro is straightforward and provides many choices for different shooting settings. Here's how to capture images and film movies using your iPhone's Camera app:

Taking Photos:

Open the Camera App: Swipe left from the lock screen or home screen, or to open the Camera app, tap its icon on your home screen.

Select a Camera Mode: Swipe horizontally on the camera interface to pick a mode (e.g., Photo, Portrait, Panorama, etc.) that meets your shooting requirements.

Frame Your Shot: Aim your iPhone toward the topic you wish to photograph. You may utilize the viewfinder on the screen to compose your shot.

Focus and Exposure: Tap the area on the screen where you wish to set the focus and exposure. Your iPhone will update the settings appropriately.

Capture the shot: Tap the white shutter button (a circle) on the screen or use the physical volume buttons to capture the image.

Examine Your Shot: After snapping the shot, you may examine it by touching the thumbnail that appears in the screen's lower left corner. From there, you may edit, share, or delete the picture.

Taking Videos:

Open the Camera App: Launch the Camera app from the lock screen or home screen.

Select the Video Mode: Swipe to the video mode by sliding horizontally on the camera interface.

Start Recording: Tap the red record button (a circle) to begin recording. While recording, you'll see a timer displaying the length of your video.

Stop Recording: To stop recording, hit the red recording button again. You'll find your video saved to the Camera Roll.

Review and Edit Videos: After recording, you may press the thumbnail that displays in the bottom-left corner to review your video. You may cut, modify, and share it from there.

Additional Tips for Photos and Videos:

HDR (High Dynamic Range): HDR may assist in capturing better-exposed images in high-contrast scenarios. You may activate or disable it in the camera settings.

Live Photos: To record Live Photos (a few seconds of video before and after capturing a picture), make sure the Live Photos icon at the top of the camera interface is set on.

Zoom: You can zoom in and out by utilizing pinch motions on the camera interface. For best quality, use the optical zoom (if available) before resorting to digital zoom.

Night Mode: If you're shooting in low-light circumstances, Night Mode will automatically activate to increase the quality of your images. Keep your phone steady throughout the capture for the best results.

Slow Motion (Slo-Mo): In the Slo-Mo mode, your iPhone captures video in slow motion. You can alter the speed of slow-motion playback in the Photos app.

Editing photographs and movies: The Photos app on your iPhone provides a variety of editing capabilities to improve your pictures and movies. After capturing, press the "Edit" button while viewing a picture or video to access these editing tools.

Experiment with multiple camera settings, explore editing possibilities and have fun capturing memories with your iPhone 15 Pro's powerful camera system.

Editing Photos

Your iPhone 15 Pro comes with a comprehensive built-in photo editor that allows you to enhance, crop, filter, and modify your photographs to create the desired style. Here's how to edit images on your iPhone:

Open the Photos App: Locate the Photos app on your home screen (it looks like a colorful flower symbol) and press it to open.

Select the picture: Browse your picture library to select the photo you want to edit and touch on it to open it.

Press "Edit": Once the picture is open, select "Edit" from the menu by clicking the button in the top-right corner. This will bring up the editing tools.

Use Editing Tools: Here are some of the editing tools and modifications you may use:

Crop & Rotate: Tap the crop icon (a square with diagonal lines) to crop or straighten the picture. You may also alter the aspect ratio.

Filters: Tap the filters icon (three overlapping circles) to add several preset filters to your shot. Swipe left or right to examine various filter styles.

Auto Enhance: Tap the magic wand symbol to add automated improvements to your shot. This may enhance overall picture quality.

Adjustments: Tap the adjustments icon (a series of sliders) to open various editing options:

Light: Adjust exposure, brightness, contrast, highlights, shadows, and more.

Color: Tweak the saturation, contrast, and cast of colors in the shot.

B&W: Create black and white photographs and regulate the strength of various color channels.

Sharpness: Enhance the sharpness of the shot.

Vignette: Add or minimize a vignette effect around the margins of the shot.

Make Adjustments: Tap the adjustment sliders, then use your finger to move left or right to modify each setting to your preference.

Compare Changes: To compare your altered picture to the original, touch and hold the edited image to view the original version, then release it to return to the edited version.

Reverse alterations: If you make changes you don't like, press "Revert" to reverse your alterations and return to the original picture.

Save Your altered picture: When you're finished with your modifications, press "Done" in the lower-right corner of the screen to save the modified version of the picture.

Duplicate and Preserve Original: If you wish to retain the original picture as well as the changed one, you may duplicate the photo before editing by hitting the share symbol and choosing "Duplicate."

Share Your altered picture: After saving your modified image, you can share it with friends and family right from the Photos app by pressing the share button.

Your iPhone's photo editor gives a wide variety of options to improve and fine-tune your images, whether you're tweaking exposure, adding filters, or cropping for a better composition. Experiment with these elements to take your images to the next level.

FaceTime and Video Calls

Apple offers video and audio calling through FaceTime that enables you to make high-quality video chats with other Apple customers. Here's how to utilize FaceTime and make video calls on your iPhone 15 Pro:

FaceTime App: Your iPhone comes with the FaceTime app pre-installed. Locate the FaceTime app on your home screen, which features a white video camera symbol with a green backdrop.

Initiating a Video Call: To make a video call using FaceTime, follow these steps:

Open the FaceTime app.

Tap the "+" button in the top-right corner.

In the "To:" area, put the contact's name, phone number, or email address. If the contact is stored in your Contacts app, you may start entering their name, and it will offer matches.

Tap the contact's name when it appears in the search results.

To start a video call, tap the icon with the video camera.

Accepting a FaceTime Call: When someone starts a FaceTime call with you, your iPhone will ring, and a notice will display on the screen. To answer the call, touch the green "Accept" button. To refuse it, press the red "refuse" button.

Making FaceTime Calls from Other Applications: You may now initiate FaceTime calls straight from other applications like Messages or Contacts. Open the chat or contact, hit the FaceTime symbol, and a video conference will commence.

Group FaceTime Conversations: FaceTime allows group video conversations, enabling you to communicate with numerous individuals simultaneously. To make a group FaceTime call, follow the same steps as before, but choose additional contacts before pressing the video camera button.

FaceTime options: Customize your FaceTime experience by navigating to "Settings" > "FaceTime." Here, you can customize options like your caller ID, whether or not you wish to enable FaceTime over cellular data, and more.

FaceTime Audio Calls: In addition to video calls, you can conduct FaceTime audio calls. To make an audio call, follow the same steps as initiating a video call, but touch the phone symbol instead of the video camera icon.

FaceTime Effects (Optional): During a FaceTime chat, you may have some fun with effects like Animoji and Memoji by touching the star-shaped symbol. This enables you to apply stickers, filters, and more to your face.

Switching Cameras: During a FaceTime chat, you may change between the front and back cameras by touching the camera symbol with arrows in a circle.

FaceTime is a wonderful method to remain connected with friends, family, and coworkers via video and voice chats. It's easy to use and delivers a smooth experience on your iPhone 15 Pro.

Apps and App Store

Apps are a vital component of your iPhone 15 Pro's functionality, enabling you to personalize your smartphone and access a wide variety of services. Here's an overview of applications and how to utilize the App Store to download and manage them:

App Store: Applications for your iPhone can be found, downloaded, and updated via the App Store. It's symbolized by a blue icon with an "A" on it. To access it, press the App Store icon on your home screen.

Browsing and Searching for Apps: In the App Store, you may explore apps by category featured apps or search for specific apps by utilizing the screen's bottom search box.

Downloading Apps: To download an app, press its icon, then hit the "Get" button (or the price if it's a paid app). It might ask for your Apple ID password or require you to use Face ID or Touch ID to authenticate yourself.

App Updates: Apps are routinely updated to include new features, upgrades, and security fixes. To update your apps:

Open the App Store.

In the upper-right corner, tap the symbol for your profile.

Scroll down to the "Pending Updates" area, then hit "Update All" or update applications individually.

App Library: The App Library is a feature introduced in iOS 14 that automatically organizes your applications into categories. You may access it by swiping left on your home screen.

Arranging Apps on the Home Screen: To rearrange apps on your home screen or create folders, press and hold an app until it begins to jiggle, then drag it to your chosen place or onto another app to form a folder.

Deleting Apps: To remove an app, press and hold its icon until it jiggles, then hit the "X" that appears in the corner of the app's icon. Confirm the deletion when requested.

App alerts: Apps may give you alerts to keep you informed. You may change notification settings for each app in "Settings" > "Notifications."

Privacy and App Permissions: Some applications may seek access to different functionalities, including location, camera, and microphone. You may modify app permissions in "Settings" > "Privacy."

App Security: iOS is developed with security in mind. They go through a review process before being approved on the App Store, and you can download them with confidence, knowing they satisfy Apple's security requirements.

In-App Purchases: Some applications offer in-app purchases for extra features or content. Make careful to read reviews and be cautious while buying in-app purchases.

App Store Subscriptions: Some applications provide subscription services. You may adjust and cancel subscriptions under "Settings" > "[Your Name]" > "Subscriptions."

Offloading Unused Applications: iOS may automatically offload applications you don't use frequently to clear up storage space. This doesn't remove your data, and the software may be reinstalled when required.

App assistance: If you have questions or need assistance with a particular app, you may visit the app's page in the App Store for contact information or visit the developer's website.

Your iPhone 15 Pro's App Store gives access to a broad ecosystem of applications that may expand your device's usefulness, from productivity tools to entertainment and beyond. Explore, download, and enjoy the applications that fit your requirements and interests.

Managing App Permissions

Your iPhone 15 Pro enables you to decide which applications have access to certain device capabilities and personal data. Here's how to manage app permissions:

Open Settings: Select the "Settings" app on your home screen. It's symbolized with a gearwheel icon.

Navigate to Privacy: Scroll down and hit "Privacy." This area allows precise control over app permissions.

Choose an App Category: You'll notice numerous categories reflecting various sorts of permissions, including Location Services, Camera, Microphone, Contacts, and more. Choose the class corresponding to the permit you wish to manage.

Review App Permissions: Within each category, A list of applications that have asked to use that specific function will be displayed. For example, under the "Location Services" area, you can see which applications have requested access to your location.

Customize Permissions: Tap on an app to view the various permission choices. Depending on the app and the permission, you may have multiple choices:

Never: The app is denied access to this feature forever.

When Using the App: This feature is only available to the app when it is actively being used.

Always: The app has unfettered access to this feature, even when it's not in use.

Adjust Permissions: To alter an app's permission, choose the option that best meets your desire (e.g., "While Using the App" or "Never"). Your modifications will be saved automatically.

Location Services: If you're managing location rights, you may now define a specific location accuracy choice for each app. Some applications may provide "Precise" (using GPS) or "Approximate" (using generic location data) choices.

App Tracking Transparency (iOS 14.5 and later): With App Tracking Transparency, you may select whether applications can follow your behavior across other firms' apps and websites. When an app asks for tracking permission, you'll see a pop-up message asking for your agreement to be monitored. You may opt to accept or ask the app not to watch you.

Background App update: In "Settings" > "General" > "Background App Refresh," you may control which applications are permitted to update information in the background. Disabling this functionality for specific applications will help preserve battery life.

Reset App Permissions: If you wish to reset all app permissions to their default settings, to accomplish this, go to "Settings" > "General" > "Reset" > "Reset Location & Privacy." Be careful since this action will reset all rights for all applications.

Notifications: In "Settings" > "Notifications," you may manage notifications for particular applications, setting when and how they can inform you.

By setting app permissions, you can safeguard your privacy and regulate which applications have access to your personal data and device functionalities. This enables you to find a balance between app usefulness and privacy on your iPhone 15 Pro.

App Store Basics

Accessing the Application Store: To access the App Store, press its icon on your home screen. The symbol displays a blue backdrop with the white letter "A."

Browsing and Searching: You may explore applications by categories like "Today," "Games," "applications," and more. To locate a certain app, utilize the search box at the bottom of the screen. You may search by app name or keywords.

Downloading Apps: To download an app, press the app's icon or name to access its information. Then, press the "Get" button (or the fee if it's a premium app). If asked, authenticate the download with Face ID, Touch ID, or your Apple ID password.

App Updates: Apps are routinely updated to give new features and fixes. To update your apps:

Open the App Store.

In the upper-right corner, tap the symbol for your profile.

Scroll down to the "Pending Updates" column and press "Update All" or update applications individually.

App Reviews and Ratings: You can read user reviews and check ratings for applications by scrolling down on their sites. This might help you decide whether to download an app.

App Details: When you touch on an app's icon or name, you'll get extensive information, screenshots, user reviews, and similar applications. You may also see the app's size and compatibility.

In-App Purchases and Subscriptions: Some applications offer in-app purchases or subscriptions for extra features or content. Be aware of this while downloading applications and make educated decisions.

App Store Account: Your App Store account is connected to your Apple ID. To access your account, hit your profile symbol in the top-right corner of the Application Store. From there, you can browse your bought applications, change payment information, and more.

App Store Settings: In your iPhone settings, under "iTunes & App Store," you may customize options, including automatic downloads, app ratings, and password preferences.

Offloading unneeded applications: If your smartphone runs short on capacity, iOS may automatically unload unnecessary applications while retaining their data. You may activate this option in "Settings" > "App Store."

App Library: iOS 14 introduced the App Library, a tool that automatically organizes your applications into categories. You may access it by swiping left on your home screen.

App Clips (iOS 14 and later): App Clips enable you to utilize a tiny chunk of an app without downloading the complete app. They are often activated by QR codes or NFC tags and allow rapid access to certain software functionalities.

Family Sharing: With Family Sharing, you can share bought applications, subscriptions, and more with family members. Set up Family Sharing in your Apple ID settings.

The App Store is your source for finding and downloading a broad choice of applications that may improve your iPhone 15 Pro's capabilities. Whether you're searching for work tools, entertainment applications, or games, the App Store provides a vast variety to discover and enjoy.

Privacy and Security

Protecting your privacy and protecting the security of your iPhone 15 Pro is vital. Apple takes privacy seriously and includes numerous options and settings to help you keep control over your data and device. Here's how to boost privacy and security:

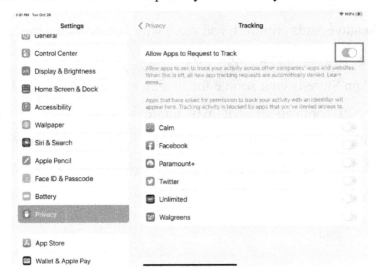

Set Up Face ID or Touch ID: To unlock your smartphone and verify app downloads, set up Face ID (facial recognition) or Touch ID (fingerprint recognition) under "Settings" > "Face ID & Passcode" or "Touch ID & Passcode."

Strong Passcode: Create a strong, alphanumeric passcode for your smartphone in case Face ID or Touch ID fails or isn't accessible. Avoid readily guessable passwords like "1234" or "0000."

Enable Two-Factor Authentication (2FA): Enable 2FA for your Apple ID to offer an additional layer of protection. It asks you to input a verification code issued to your trusted devices or phone number when checking in on new devices.

App Permissions: Review and manage app permissions to control which applications may access features like location, camera, and microphone. Go to "Options" > "Privacy" to adjust these options.

App Tracking Transparency (iOS 14.5 and later): With App Tracking Transparency, applications require your permission to follow your behavior across other firms' apps and websites. You may opt to accept or refuse tracking requests.

Find My iPhone: Enable "Find My iPhone" under "Settings" > "[Your Name]" > "Find My" to locate, lock, or wipe your smartphone remotely if it's lost or stolen.

Automatic App Updates: Ensure that your applications are constantly up to date by activating automatic app updates in "Settings" > "App Store."

Strong, Unique Passwords: Make sure your account passwords are strong and distinct. You may use the built-in Password Manager or a third-party password manager tool to create and store passwords securely.

Data Encryption: Your iPhone encrypts your data by default. Ensure that you have a secure device passcode, and your data will be encrypted while saved and delivered.

Safari Privacy Features: Safari has numerous privacy features, like Intelligent Tracking Prevention to prevent cross-site tracking. Explore Safari options under "options" > "Safari" to change your privacy choices.

App Store Security: Only download programs from the official App Store since Apple carefully evaluates and authorizes apps for security. Avoid sideloading programs from unknown sources.

Family Sharing: If you use Family Sharing, establish permissions and limitations for family members' devices to preserve your family's privacy.

Regular Software upgrades: Keep your smartphone up to speed with the newest iOS upgrades. These upgrades generally contain security patches and improvements.

Emergency SOS and Medical ID: Set up Emergency SOS and fill out your Medical ID in the Health app (available from the emergency call screen) to offer crucial information in case of crises.

Wi-Fi and Network Security: Be careful while connecting to public Wi-Fi networks. Consider utilizing a VPN for enhanced protection, particularly while on unknown networks.

By following these privacy and security standards, you can guarantee that your iPhone 15 Pro maintains a safe and private environment for your data and information. Apple's dedication to user privacy means you have tools and capabilities at your disposal to secure your digital life.

Face ID/Touch ID (If appropriate) and Passcode and Security Settings

Face ID and Touch ID are biometric authentication systems that enable a simple and safe way to unlock your iPhone and authenticate different tasks. Here's how to set up and maintain Face ID/Touch ID and alter security settings:

Setting Up Face ID/Touch ID

When you initially set up your iPhone 15 Pro, you'll have the choice to set Face ID (if available) or Touch ID (if you have an earlier model without Face ID):

Face ID: Follow the on-screen directions to scan your face by moving it inside the prescribed frame. Once setup is complete, your smartphone will utilize Face ID for authentication.

Touch ID: Your finger should be on the Home button (earlier models) or the Power button (iPhone 15 Pro and after) repeatedly until your device successfully detects your fingerprint.

Passcode: Regardless of whether you use Face ID or Touch ID, it's vital to set up a passcode as a backup authentication option. To establish or update your passcode:

Open "Settings."

Scroll down and touch "Face ID & Passcode" (or "Touch ID & Passcode" on earlier smartphones).

Enter your existing passcode if asked.

Tap "Change Passcode" or "Turn Passcode On" if it's not currently enabled.

Follow the on-screen steps to generate a passcode. You may pick between a bespoke alphanumeric code, a 4-digit code, or a 6-digit code.

Enabling/Disabling Face ID/Touch ID: To activate or disable Face ID or Touch ID for certain tasks (e.g., unlocking your iPhone, making purchases), go to "Settings" > "Face ID & Passcode" (or "Touch ID & Passcode") and enter your passcode. You may then turn the different features on or off.

Require Passcode: Under "Settings" > "Face ID & Passcode" (or "Touch ID & Passcode"), you may set when your iPhone requires a passcode. Options include "Immediately," "After 1 minute," "After 5 minutes," etc.

Erase Data: In the "Face ID & Passcode" (or "Touch ID & Passcode") settings, you may activate "Erase Data." This option erases all data on your smartphone after ten failed passcode tries, boosting security.

Attention Aware Features (Face ID Only): If you want Face ID to demand your attention for it to operate (e.g., open your eyes), ensure that "Attention Aware Features" is activated in the Face ID settings.

Alternate look (Face ID Only): If you wish to add an alternate look for Face ID (e.g., wearing sunglasses), you may do so under the Face ID settings.

Passcode Changes: You may change your passcode at any moment by navigating to "Settings" > "Face ID & Passcode" (or "Touch ID & Passcode") and choosing "Change Passcode."

Lost or Stolen Device: If you misplace or have your iPhone stolen, take advantage of Find My iPhone to locate, lock, or wipe your device remotely for added security. You may access this capability through iCloud or the Find My app.

By configuring Face ID/Touch ID and passcode settings, you can guarantee your iPhone 15 Pro stays both safe and comfortable for regular usage. These features give an extra degree of safety for your device and data.

Privacy Settings

Your iPhone 15 Pro features different privacy options that enable you to regulate how your data is collected and used by applications and services. Here's how to adjust privacy settings:

Location Services: Go to "Settings" > "Privacy" > "Location Services" to examine and manage which applications have access to your location. You may change individual app permissions to "Never," "While Using the App," or "Always."

App monitoring Transparency (iOS 14.5 and later): This feature asks applications to obtain your permission before monitoring your activities across other firms' apps and websites. Manage this option under "Settings" > "Privacy" > "Tracking."

Microphone and Camera Access: Under "Settings" > "Privacy," you can examine which applications have requested access to your microphone and camera. Control these rights on a per-app basis.

Contacts, Calendars, and Reminders: In "Settings" > "Privacy," you can see which applications have requested access to your contacts, calendars, and reminders. Adjust these permissions for each app separately.

Images: Review and regulate which applications have access to your images under "Settings" > "Privacy" > "Photos." applications may request access to all photos or just selected albums.

Bluetooth: Manage Bluetooth permissions for applications under "Settings" > "Privacy" > "Bluetooth."

Health: Control which applications have access to your health data and settings under "Settings" > "Privacy" > "Health."

Motion & Fitness: In "Settings" > "Privacy," you can see which applications have requested access to motion and fitness data. Adjust permissions for each app.

Background App Refresh: Under "Settings" > "Privacy," you may check and manage which applications are authorized to refresh information in the background. Disabling this for specific applications may preserve battery life.

HomeKit: Manage your HomeKit settings for home automation and smart devices under "Settings" > "Privacy" > "HomeKit."

Media & Apple Music: In "Settings" > "Privacy," you can evaluate which applications have sought access to your media collection and modify these rights.

Advertising: Limit ad tracking by heading to "Settings" > "Privacy" > "Advertising" and setting "Limit Ad Tracking." You can also reset your advertising identification here.

App Privacy Report (iOS 15 and later): The App Privacy Report gives insights into how applications utilize your data. You can view it by selecting "Settings" > "Privacy" > "App Privacy Report."

Siri & Search: Manage Siri and search recommendations under "Settings" > "Privacy" > "Siri & Search." You may select which applications can use Siri and remove your Siri and Dictation history.

Location-Based Alerts: Under "Settings" > "Privacy" > "Location Services," you may allow or disable location-based alerts and notifications for applications.

Share My Location: Share your location with family and friends using "Find My" and "Find My Friends" by heading to "Settings" > "[Your Name]" > "Find My" > "Share My Location."

Share Across Devices: Control whether applications and services may share data across your Apple devices under "Settings" > "[Your Name]" > "Find My" > "Share My Location."

Reset Privacy Settings: If you wish to reset all privacy settings to their default values, you may do so under "Settings" > "General" > "Reset" > "Reset private Settings." Be careful since this action will affect all private settings.

Managing these privacy settings allows you to preserve your personal information and regulate how applications and services interact with your data on your iPhone 15 Pro. Review and update these options to accord with your privacy choices.

Battery and Charging

To get the most out of your iPhone 15 Pro's battery life and preserve its health, consider the following recommendations for effective charging and battery management:

Use genuine Accessories: Always use genuine Apple accessories, including the charger and cord, to guarantee safe and efficient charging.

Avoid Extreme Temperatures: Keep your iPhone within the recommended temperature range (0°C to 35°C or 32°F to 95°F) to preserve battery health.

Enable Optimized Battery Charging: In "Settings" > "Battery" > "Battery Health," enable "Optimized Battery Charging." This function helps decrease the wear and tear on your battery by learning your regular charging practices.

Use Low Power Mode: Activate Low Power Mode when your battery is going low. It lowers background activities and enhances battery life.

Reduce Screen Brightness: Lower your screen brightness or activate auto-brightness in "Settings" > "Display & Brightness" to preserve power.

Manage Background App Refresh: Go to "Settings" > "General" > "Background App Refresh" and deactivate it for applications that don't need to update in the background.

Close Unused Applications: Manually close applications running in the background to prevent them from using power. Swipe up from the bottom of the screen (or swipe up and hold on iPhone X and later) and swipe away applications.

Check Battery Usage: Monitor which applications are using the most battery power under "Settings" > "Battery." If you detect any apps using excessive power, try modifying their settings or shutting them when not in use.

Use Wi-Fi Over Cellular Data: When feasible, connect to Wi-Fi networks instead of utilizing cellular data since Wi-Fi is often more power-efficient.

Disable Push Email: Set your email accounts to retrieve new messages manually or less regularly to limit the frequency of data fetching.

Enable Low Data Mode: In "Settings" > "Cellular," enable Low Data Mode to limit data use and increase battery life.

Turn Off Unnecessary Location Services: In "Settings" > "Privacy" > "Location Services," evaluate which applications have access to your location and alter permissions appropriately.

Turn Off Dynamic Wallpapers: Use static wallpapers instead of dynamic or live wallpapers to preserve power.

Update iOS: Keep your iPhone's operating system up to date. Apple routinely provides updates with battery optimizations and bug fixes.

Battery Replacement: If your battery health lowers drastically, consider obtaining a battery replacement from an authorized service provider.

Wireless Charging: You may charge your iPhone wirelessly with a suitable Qi-certified charger. It's handy and minimizes wear on the charging port.

Overnight Charging: Avoid keeping your iPhone plugged in and charging overnight. Unplug it when it reaches 100% to avoid overcharging.

By following these techniques, you can improve the battery life of your iPhone 15 Pro and keep it working effectively. Remember that battery health naturally diminishes over time, but following techniques may help extend its longevity.

Pro Camera Modes and ProRAW and ProRes Video

The iPhone 15 Pro delivers sophisticated camera capabilities, including Pro Camera Modes, ProRAW, and ProRes video, to help you produce professional-quality images and movies. Here's an overview of these features:

Pro Camera Modes:

Manual Exposure Control: With Pro Camera Modes, you have complete manual control over parameters like ISO, shutter speed, and focus. This enables you to alter exposure and produce unique photographic effects.

Adjustable White Balance: You may fine-tune white balance settings to get accurate color representation under diverse lighting circumstances.

RAW shoot: Pro Camera Modes lets you shoot photographs in RAW format, retaining maximum image quality and allowing you greater freedom in post-processing.

Live Histogram: The live histogram delivers real-time feedback on your exposure, helping you produce well-balanced photos.

Focus Peaking: This function shows the parts of your shot that are in focus, facilitating fine manual focus changes.

Manual Focus: You may manually change the focus point to produce the appropriate depth of field or creative effects.

Pro Camera Grid: Use gridlines to align your photographs and generate well-composed photos.

ProRAW: ProRAW is a file format that combines the freedom of RAW picture capture with the computational photography capabilities of the iPhone. It lets you take photographs with all the data from the camera sensor, allowing you greater control during post-processing. Here's how to utilize ProRAW:

Open the Camera app.

Swipe to the "Pro" mode.

Tap the "RAW" symbol to activate ProRAW capture.

Take your shot, and it will be stored in ProRAW format alongside a conventional JPEG.

ProRes Video: ProRes is a high-quality video codec created by Apple. It's commonly used in professional video production. The iPhone 15 Pro supports ProRes video recording, enabling you to create high-quality footage with stunning color and detail. Here's how to utilize ProRes video:

Open the Camera app.

Swipe to the "Video" mode.

Tap the resolution and frame rate options.

Choose the "ProRes" option (if available). You may pick between ProRes 422 and ProRes 422 HQ for various degrees of quality.

Start filming your video.

Keep in mind that ProRes video files are bigger than ordinary video formats, so you'll need adequate storage space. Additionally, you may need more complex video editing tools to harness the advantages of ProRes properly.

These Pro Camera Modes, ProRAW, and ProRes video capabilities allow you to elevate your photography and filmmaking to a professional level with your iPhone 15 Pro. Explore these settings and explore to unlock your creativity.

Dolby Vision Video Recording

The iPhone 15 Pro features Dolby Vision video recording, offering you the opportunity to produce beautiful, cinematic-quality footage. Here's an introduction to how to utilize Dolby Vision and what it offers:

What is Dolby Vision: Dolby Vision is an improved high dynamic range (HDR) technology used in video production and playback. It increases the quality of films by delivering higher contrast, brighter highlights, and more vibrant colors.

How to Enable Dolby Vision Video Recording:

Open the Camera app on your iPhone 15 Pro.

Swipe to the "Video" mode.

In the video mode, you'll find choices for resolution and frame rate. To activate Dolby Vision, pick one of the Dolby Vision choices (usually labeled as "Dolby Vision 4K @ 30fps" or equivalent, depending on your area).

Start filming your video.

Benefits of Dolby Vision Video Recording:

Enhanced Dynamic Range: Dolby Vision records a larger range of brightness levels, from deep blacks to dazzling highlights, resulting in more realistic and colorful films.

Improved Color Accuracy: Dolby Vision gives more accurate and true-to-life colors, making your films more appealing.

Professional-Like Quality: With Dolby Vision, your iPhone 15 Pro can generate video quality that's equivalent to professional cameras and editing processes.

Editing Dolby Vision Videos:

To fully leverage the advantages of Dolby Vision, you'll want to edit your movies with software that supports Dolby Vision. Here's how to deal with Dolby Vision videos:

Transfer Videos: Transfer your Dolby Vision videos to your computer via iCloud, AirDrop, or a USB cord.

Edit Software: Use video editing software that supports Dolby Vision, such as Final Cut Pro X, Adobe Premiere Pro, or iMovie on macOS.

Color Grading: Dolby Vision films enable accurate color grading and correction to get the desired cinematic effect.

Export: When exporting your modified video, ensure that you use the Dolby Vision format to retain the expanded dynamic range and color fidelity.

Remember that Dolby Vision movies tend to have bigger file sizes owing to the greater quality, so make sure you have appropriate storage space on your device.

By utilizing Dolby Vision video recording on your iPhone 15 Pro and editing incompatible software, you can produce remarkable, professional-quality films with breathtaking graphics and color accuracy.

Troubleshooting and Tips

While your iPhone 15 Pro is a strong and dependable smartphone, you may find occasional glitches or wish to enhance its performance. Here are some troubleshooting techniques and beneficial suggestions:

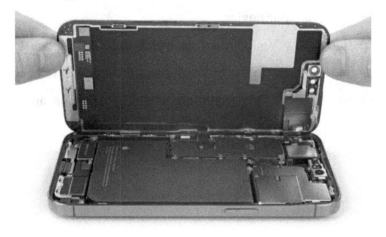

Restart Your iPhone: If you have small troubles, consider restarting your iPhone by turning it off and then back on. This may fix many temporary issues.

Software upgrades: Ensure that your iPhone has the latest iOS upgrades. Apple constantly provides updates with bug fixes and upgrades. To view the latest updates, select "Settings" > "General" > "Update of Software."

Free Up Storage: Insufficient storage might damage your iPhone's performance. Delete unneeded programs, images, and movies, or consider relocating them to iCloud or an external storage option.

Clear App Cache: Some applications may retain temporary data that might build over time. Clear app caches by removing and reinstalling applications or checking whether particular apps provide cache-clearing alternatives.

Reset Settings: If you face persistent troubles, you may reset all settings without losing your data. Go to "Settings" > "General" > "Reset" > "Reset All Settings."

Troubleshoot connection: If you have troubles with Wi-Fi or cellular connection, turn Airplane Mode on and off, restart your router, or contact your service provider for help.

Battery Optimization: To enhance battery life, utilize Low Power Mode when your battery is running low and adjust background app refresh and location services in settings.

Touch Screen Issues: If your touch screen is unresponsive, wipe it with a microfiber cloth and check you don't have a screen protector or case interfering with touch sensitivity.

Face ID/Touch ID Troubleshooting: If Face ID or Touch ID isn't functioning correctly, check your device's sensors and your face/finger are clean. You may also reset Face ID or Touch ID in settings if required.

App Issues: If an app is malfunctioning or crashing, try force-quitting the app, upgrading it, or reinstalling it from the App Store.

Backup Regularly: Make frequent backups of your iPhone using iCloud or iTunes/Finder on your PC. This assures you can recover your data in case of any errors.

Contact Apple Support: If you're unable to address a problem on your own, don't hesitate to contact Apple Support for help or Make an appointment at an authorized repair provider or the Apple Store.

Security Awareness: Stay cautious about your device's security. Avoid clicking on dodgy links or installing programs from unknown sources.

Use Screen Time: Screen Time in settings enables you to monitor and regulate your screen time and app use. Use it to establish restrictions and manage your digital well-being.

Privacy Settings: Review and update privacy settings to secure your data. See the "Privacy Settings" section of this guide for more. Remember that many difficulties may be handled with easy troubleshooting. Still, if you have hardware problems or persistent software issues, it's best to get help from Apple or an authorized service provider. Regularly servicing your iPhone 15 Pro and keeping it up to date can assist in guaranteeing a smooth and trouble-free experience.

Common Issues and Solutions and Tips for Better Performance

Here are some frequent difficulties you may find with your iPhone 15 Pro, along with strategies to remedy them:

Battery Draining Quickly:

Solution: Check for applications operating in the background, use Low Power Mode when required, and optimize battery settings. If the problem continues, try checking for battery health in "Settings" > "Battery" > "Battery Health," or in case a replacement battery is needed, get in touch with an authorized service provider or the Apple Store.

Slow Performance

Solution: Close background applications, delete app caches, and check you have the latest iOS upgrades. If performance difficulties continue, consider resetting all settings (Settings > General > Reset > Reset All Settings). Back up your files before doing this.

Wi-Fi or Cellular Connection Problems:

Solution: Restart your smartphone, turn Airplane Mode on and off, reset network settings (Settings > General > Reset > Reset Network Settings), and check you're running the newest iOS version. If troubles continue, contact your service provider or Apple Support.

App Crashes or Freezes:

Solution: Update applications to the newest versions from the App Store. If an app continues to crash, consider removing and reinstalling it. If it's a system app creating troubles, try resetting all settings (as indicated before).

Face ID/Touch ID Not Working:

Solution: Ensure your face/finger and the device's sensors are clean. Reset Face ID or Touch ID if required (Configuration > Touch ID & Passcode or Face ID & Passcode). Also, consider upgrading your iOS version.

Unresponsive Touch Screen:

Solution: Clean the screen using a microfiber cloth, check there's no interference from screen protectors or cases, and then restart your device.

No Sound or Low Volume:

Solution: Check the physical mute switch on the side of your iPhone. Ensure sound is not muted in settings. If difficulties persist, restart your device and try plugging in and unplugging headphones.

App Store Issues:

Solution: Check your internet connection, log out of the App Store and back into your Apple ID, and try emptying the App Store cache by clicking the "Today" button 10 times.

Tips for Better Performance:

Regularly Update iOS: Keep your iPhone updated to the newest iOS version for bug fixes and performance improvements.

Manage Background programs: Manually close programs operating in the background to save system resources.

Use Low Power Mode: Activate Low Power Mode to preserve the battery as required.

Clear App Caches: Some applications may contain caches that eat storage. Delete and reinstall programs or clean their caches as required.

Free Up Storage: Regularly remove useless programs, photographs, and videos to free up storage space.

Adjust Settings: Review and adjust settings like location services, notifications, and background app refresh to increase battery life and performance.

Protect Your Device: Put on a screen guard and case to protect your iPhone from physical harm.

Regular Backups: Back up your iPhone often to guarantee you don't lose essential data.

App Management: Keep your applications up to date and uninstall unneeded ones to clean your smartphone.

Privacy and Security:

- Stay cautious about privacy and security.

- Avoid unfamiliar connections.

- Activate two-factor authentication for enhanced protection.

By fixing frequent problems and following these performance guidelines, you can keep your iPhone 15 Pro in peak condition and enjoy a smoother user experience.

Updates and Maintenance

Software Updates: iOS Updates: Check for iOS updates frequently to maintain the smooth and secure operation of your device. To view the latest updates, select "Settings" > "General" > "Update of Software.

App Updates: App Store: Keep your applications up to date by activating automatic app updates in the App Store settings or manually upgrading apps when informed.

Backup Your Data: Regularly backup your iPhone using iCloud or iTunes/Finder on your PC. This guarantees your data is protected in case of device loss or failure.

Optimize Storage:

Clear unneeded applications: Delete unnecessary applications to save up storage space.

Delete Old Photos and Videos: Remove old media files or transfer them to iCloud or external storage.

Offload Unused Apps: Enable the "Offload Unused Apps" option in "Settings" > "General" > "iPhone Storage" to automatically delete apps you don't regularly use while saving their data.

Battery Maintenance: Optimized Battery Charging: Enable this function in "Settings" > "Battery" > "Battery Health" to improve your battery's lifetime.

Monitor Battery Health: Periodically check your battery's health under the same "Battery Health" area. If it's considerably impaired, consider having a battery replacement from an authorized service provider.

Clean Your iPhone: Use a microfiber cloth to clean your iPhone's screen and body frequently. Avoid using abrasive items or cleaning products.

Privacy and Security: Review and update privacy settings to restrict how applications access your data. Enable two-factor authentication for enhanced security.

Keep It Protected: Use a screen protector and a protective case to safeguard your iPhone from physical harm.

Wi-Fi and Cellular Data: Connect to reputable Wi-Fi networks whenever feasible to preserve cellular data. Be careful while using public Wi-Fi networks, and consider utilizing a VPN for enhanced protection.

Reset Settings (As Needed): If you notice persistent troubles, try resetting settings without losing your data. Go to "Settings" > "General" > "Reset" > "Reset All Settings."

Regular Maintenance Schedule: Establish a regular maintenance regimen for your iPhone, such as weekly or monthly, to guarantee it's working correctly.

By following these steps, you can guarantee that your iPhone 15 Pro is updated, safe, and well-maintained, providing you with a dependable and delightful user experience. Regular maintenance may increase the life of your gadget and help avoid frequent faults.

Software Updates and Backing Up Your Phone

Keeping your iPhone 15 Pro's software up to date is critical for several reasons, including speed improvements, new features, and security updates. Here's how to handle software updates:

Automatic upgrades: Your iPhone can automatically download and install iOS upgrades. To activate this option, go to "Settings" > "General" > "Software Update" > "Download iOS updates automatically."

Manual Updates: To manually check for updates, go to "Settings" > "General" > "Software Update." Install any available updates by following the on-screen instructions for download and installation.

Install Updates Overnight: You may schedule iOS updates to install over the night while your smartphone is charged and connected to Wi-Fi. When an update is ready, hit "Install Tonight" when asked.

iOS Update Notifications: iOS will alert you when a new update is ready. You may choose to "Install" it immediately or "Later" to plan the update for a more convenient time.

Backing Up Your iPhone 15 Pro:

Regularly backing up your iPhone guarantees that your data is protected and can be retrieved in case of device loss, damage, or other difficulties. Here are your backup options:

iCloud Backup: iCloud offers a simple and quick solution to back up your iPhone wirelessly. To activate iCloud Backup:

Go to "Settings" > [your name] > "iCloud."

Tap "iCloud Backup."

Toggle on "iCloud Backup."

Tap "Back Up Now" to begin an instant backup.

iCloud backups of your iPhone will happen automatically while connected to Wi-Fi, locked, and plugged in. It contains your photographs, movies, app data, device settings, and more.

iTunes/Finder Backup: You can also generate a backup of your iPhone on your computer using iTunes (on macOS Catalina and older) or Finder (on macOS Big Sur and after). Here's how:

To link your iPhone and PC, use a USB cord.

Open iTunes or Finder (depending on your macOS version).

Select your device when it displays.

In the "General" tab, click "Back Up Now."

Automatic iCloud Backups: Ensure that iCloud Backup is activated (as described above). iCloud will automatically back up your device while connected to Wi-Fi, plugged in, and locked. Backups occur every day as long as specific requirements are satisfied.

Manual iCloud Backups: To manually launch an iCloud backup, go to "Settings" > [your name] > "iCloud" > "iCloud Backup" > "Back Up Now."

Manage Backups: You can see and manage your backups under "Settings" > [your name] > "iCloud" > "Manage Storage" > "Backups." Here, you can remove old backups or check when the last backup happened.

Remember to back up your iPhone often, particularly before significant software changes or before obtaining a new device. This guarantees that your data stays secure and accessible when you need it.

Accessibility Features and Accessibility Settings

VoiceOver: A screen reader offering spoken commentary.

Magnifier: Turns your iPhone into a magnifying glass.

Display & Text Size: Adjust text size, display zoom, and more.

Color Filters: Customize display colors for visual impairments.

Invert Colors and Smart Invert: Alter color schemes for readability.

Voice Control: Control your iPhone with voice commands.

Touch Accommodations: Adjust touch settings.

AssistiveTouch: On-screen touch controls.

Switch Control: Control utilizing external switches or gestures.

Siri and Dictation: Use voice commands and speech-to-text.

Subtitles and Captioning: Customize closed captions.

Hearing Devices: Connect and adjust hearing aids.

Braille Display: Connect and configure Braille displays.

Accessibility Shortcut: Enable rapid access to accessibility features.

Accessibility Keyboard: On-screen keyboard for accessibility.

Back Tap (iOS 14 and later): Perform custom actions with back taps.

Spoken Content: Enable spoken content for specific text.

These features are meant to make your iPhone more accessible and user-friendly for persons with impairments or particular requirements.

VoiceOver, Magnifier, and AssistiveTouch

Here's a quick description of VoiceOver, Magnifier, and AssistiveTouch, three crucial accessibility features on your iPhone 15 Pro:

VoiceOver:

What it does: VoiceOver is a screen reader that delivers spoken commentary for anything on your screen. It reads aloud text, buttons, icons, and other features, making your iPhone usable for persons with visual impairments.

How to enable it: You may activate VoiceOver under "Settings" > "Accessibility" > "VoiceOver."

Magnifier:

What it does: The Magnifier function transforms your iPhone into a magnifying glass, enabling you to zoom in on text, objects, or photographs. This is excellent for persons with limited eyesight or those who need to see minute details.

How to enable it: You may activate Magnifier under "Settings" > "Accessibility" > "Magnifier."

AssistiveTouch:

What it does: AssistiveTouch offers an on-screen touch interface for operating your iPhone. It's beneficial for folks with motor disabilities or those who find physical button pushes problematic.

How to activate it: You may enable AssistiveTouch under "Settings" > "Accessibility" > "Touch" > "AssistiveTouch."

These features boost the accessibility and usefulness of your iPhone, making it more inclusive for persons with varied needs and abilities.

Additional Resources

Apple's Official iPhone Support Page:

Apple Support: Apple's official support website contains thorough tips, articles, and videos covering a wide variety of subjects pertaining to iPhone use, troubleshooting, and accessibility.

iOS User Guide:

iOS User Guide: Apple provides an online user guide that covers numerous elements of iOS, including capabilities particular to the iPhone 15 Pro.

Apple Accessibility Resources:

Accessibility on iOS: Learn more about the many accessibility tools available on iOS devices, including VoiceOver, Magnifier, and more.

Accessibility Apps and Accessories:

Accessibility Apps in the App Store: Explore a selected collection of accessibility apps designed to improve the iPhone experience for people with various requirements.

Accessibility Accessories: Discover hardware accessories and gadgets that may complement your iPhone's accessibility capabilities.

Apple Support Communities: Apple Support Communities: Connect with other iPhone users and professionals to ask questions, share experiences, and seek answers to particular concerns.

YouTube Tutorials: Search YouTube for video tutorials and instructions on different iPhone 15 Pro features, tips, and techniques. Many content developers offer useful and educational videos.

The authorized service provider or local Apple Store: If you have particular questions or need in-person support, consider visiting an Apple Store or an authorized service provider. They may give individual help and direction.

These resources can help you explore further your iPhone 15 Pro's capabilities, accessibility features, and methods to maximize your user experience. Whether you're a newbie or an experienced iPhone user, there's always something new to learn and discover.

Glossary For iPhone 15 Pro

iOS: The operating system that runs on all Apple mobile devices, including the iPhone 15 Pro.

App: Short for "application," it's a software program created for certain duties or operations, such as texting, navigation, or picture editing.

Siri: Apple's virtual assistant that listens to voice requests and does things like sending messages, making reminders, or answering inquiries.

iCloud: Apple's cloud storage and synchronization service that enables you to store images, documents, and backups online and access them from numerous devices.

Face ID: A face recognition technology used to unlock your iPhone 15 Pro, make safe payments, and access applications and functions.

Touch ID: A fingerprint recognition mechanism used to unlock your smartphone and allow app purchases or payments.

Retina Display: Apple's high-resolution display technology is noted for its sharpness, clarity, and color accuracy.

3D Touch: A feature that recognizes the pressure exerted on the screen, allowing for varying degrees of interaction with applications and menus.

Haptic Touch: A feature that offers tactile feedback when you long-press on the screen or certain components, allowing rapid access to context menus.

Airdrop: A function that permits the wireless transmission of images, movies, and data between neighboring Apple devices.

iMessage: Apple's messaging service enables users to send text messages, images, videos, and more to other Apple device users through Wi-Fi or cellular data.

Control Center: A panel that allows rapid access to critical settings, such as Wi-Fi, Bluetooth, brightness, and music playing.

Notification Center: A location where you can monitor and control your alerts, accessible by sliding down from the top of the screen.

App Store: Apple's digital distribution mechanism for downloading and updating applications and games.

Widget: A little app-like component that gives fast information or shortcuts on the home screen.

Emoji: Small symbols and characters used to express emotions or communicate information in texts.

Portrait Mode: A camera function that generates a depth-of-field effect, blurring the backdrop to make the subject stand out.

iCloud Backup: Automatic backups of your device's data, settings, and app data to iCloud.

Safari: Apple's web browser for surfing the internet on your iPhone.

Privacy Settings: Options that let you govern how applications access and utilize your data, increasing your privacy and security.

AirPods: Apple's wireless earphones that allow seamless communication with your iPhone 15 Pro.

Dolby Vision: An advanced high dynamic range (HDR) technology used for collecting and presenting video with better color and contrast.

ProRAW and ProRes Video: Professional-level picture and video formats that provide better control and quality for creative content development.

Back Tap: A feature introduced in iOS 14 that enables users to initiate particular tasks by double or triple touching the back of their iPhone.

iOS Update: Regular software updates offered by Apple to enhance features, security, and performance on your device.

Conclusion

Congratulations! You've reached the end of our detailed tutorial on using your iPhone 15 Pro. We've covered everything from getting started with your new smartphone to understanding advanced features and accessibility choices. Whether you're a newbie iPhone user or an experienced expert, this tutorial has been a beneficial resource for you.

Your iPhone 15 Pro is not just a phone; it's a powerful tool that can boost your productivity, creativity, and connection. With its gorgeous display, sophisticated camera capabilities, and the newest iOS features, you have the world at your fingertips.

Remember to explore, experiment, and make this gadget your own. Customize it to fit your requirements, discover new applications and features, and remain up to speed with software upgrades for the best possible experience.

If you ever need help or have questions, remember the vast tools given by Apple, including official support, user manuals, and the friendly Apple community. Your iPhone 15 Pro is meant to be straightforward, but there's always more to discover and experience

iPhone 15 Pro Phone Guide

Thank you for picking the iPhone 15 Pro, and we wish you many pleasurable and productive times with your smartphone. Remain connected, remain creative, and stay inspired.

If you ever need more help or have further questions, don't hesitate to contact Apple Support or go back to this tutorial for reference.

Happy discovering and utilizing your iPhone 15 Pro!

www.ingramcontent.com/pod-product-compliance
Lightning Source LLC
Chambersburg PA
CBHW071251050326
40690CB00011B/2352

* 9 7 9 8 8 7 1 2 6 9 8 2 4 *